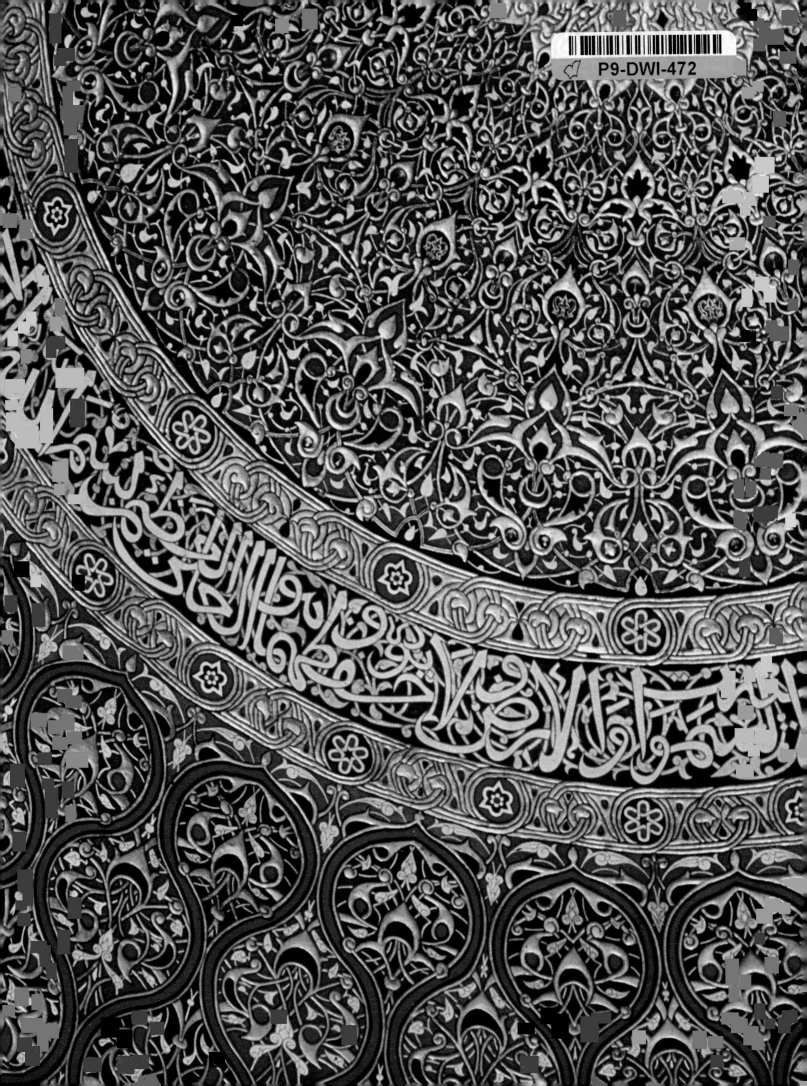

Dr. Arthur O. Stein
956 Redmond Avenue
San Jose, Calif. 95120

Dr. Arthur O. Stein
956 Redmond Avenue
San Jose, Calif. 95120

WONDERS OF MAN

DOME OF THE ROCK

by Jerry M. Landay

and the Editors
of the Newsweek Book Division

NEWSWEEK, New York

NEWSWEEK BOOK DIVISION

JOSEPH L. GARDNER   *Editor*

Janet Czarnetzki   *Art Director*

Edwin D. Bayrd, Jr.   *Associate Editor*
Laurie P. Phillips   *Picture Editor*
Eva Galan   *Assistant Editor*
Lynne H. Brown   *Copy Editor*
Russell Ash   *European Correspondent*

S. ARTHUR DEMBNER   *Publisher*

WONDERS OF MAN

MILTON GENDEL   *Consulting Editor*

Opposite:
*This panel of vibrantly colored Persian tiles
sheathes an exterior wall of the Dome of the Rock.*
Title page:
*Astride his winged steed, al-Burak, the Prophet
Mohammed ascends to Heaven. Below him lie both
Jerusalem's sacred rock (left) and Mecca's Kaaba
(right), which houses the fabled Black Stone. In
accordance with Moslem custom, the Prophet's
features are obscured by a white veil.*

ISBN: Clothbound Edition 0–88225–018–3
ISBN: Deluxe Edition 0–88225–019–1
Library of Congress Catalog Card No. 76–178707
© 1972–Arnoldo Mondadori Editore, S.p.A.

Contents

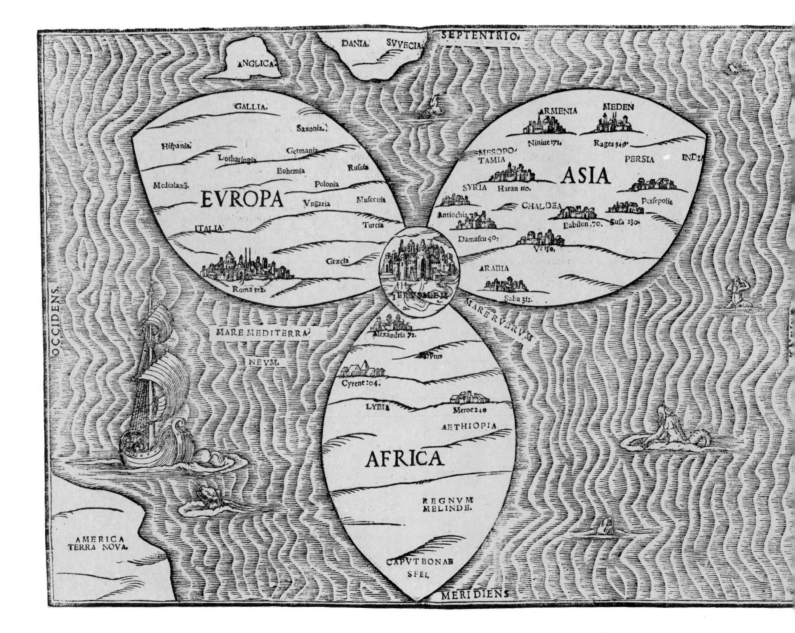

Introduction

Through an extraordinary conjunction of mythologies, the plot of land upon which the Dome of the Rock now stands is hallowed by the world's three major monotheistic religions — Judaism, Christianity, and Islam. Their conflicting claims upon the Haram Ash-Sharif, as the elevated stone platform surrounding the Dome is known, have made it the chief focus of a bitter and protracted contest of arms, one that has yet to be fully resolved. In a very real sense, Old Jerusalem and the Haram stand at the spiritual epicenter of the world — a verity emphasized by the sixteenth-century German map at left, which shows the Holy Land as the crossroads of three continents — Africa, Asia, and Europe.

Initially, it was the children of the Exodus who consecrated the site upon which the Dome was later erected. According to Jewish tradition, Abraham had offered to sacrifice his son, Isaac, upon a rock that protruded from the center of the platform — and Solomon later erected his ill-fated Temple upon the leveled plateau. For Christians, who shared the Jews' Old Testament heritage, the Temple Mount was additionally revered for its associations with the youth, ministry, and temptation of Jesus. Finally, the rock itself was sanctified for all Moslems by the famous tale of the Prophet Mohammed's Night Journey to Jerusalem. According to that durable and highly popular legend, the Prophet began his phantasmagoric ascent to Heaven from atop the scarred and pitted rock.

In the seventh century A.D. Mohammed's followers constructed a glittering gold and mosaic octagon over the rock, but the Moslems' power-base proved less durable than their shrine. Less than five centuries later the Dome of the Rock was reconsecrated the Templum Domini by the soldiers of the First Crusade — men whose bloody victory was to touch off a new era of intense political turmoil in the Middle East. Indeed, the flame of *jihad,* or holy war, flickered across Palestine for centuries to come — to the point where interminable strife became a fact of life in Old Jerusalem. Subjected to repeated military assaults over the years, the ancient walled city developed a special resiliency and character that mark it today as one of the most truly international and genuinely ecumenical communities on earth.

THE EDITORS

A HISTORY
OF JERUSALEM

I

Thrice-holy Rock

Early in the seventh century, reports of curious stirrings among the Bedouin tribes of the remote and inhospitable Arabian peninsula reached the ears of Emperor Heraclius, Augustus of Imperial Rome and Defender of Christendom's vast Eastern realm, the Byzantine Empire. The emperor was in no position to appreciate their portent, however, for he was fully occupied in a desperate struggle to stave off disaster from the east. The Sassanid Persians led by Khosrau II had recently swept across Byzantine territory, capturing Syria, winning control of Asia Minor, and encamping on the shores of the narrow Bosporus — across from the very walls of Heraclius's capital, Constantinople. They pushed south through Palestine to Sinai and Egypt, putting Jerusalem to the sword in 614.

The Christian world could scarcely believe the news. The Persians had butchered 60,000 Christians in the Holy City and sold 35,000 into slavery. Churches and shrines had been demolished — including the most revered of the holy places, the Church of the Holy Sepulcher, built in 335 over the traditional site of Jesus' Crucifixion and Resurrection. Moreover, the Persians had carried off to their capital at Ctesiphon on the banks of the Tigris the Patriarch of Jerusalem, Zacharias, together with the most hallowed relics of Christendom: the True Cross, the Crown of Thorns, and the Cup of the Last Supper.

The war dragged on for nineteen years, draining the resources of the two empires. At last, in 622, Heraclius swung to the offensive. He cleared Asia Minor and Syria, and by 628 he was advancing on Ctesiphon itself. In the midst of these events, envoys arrived at the courts of the two warring monarchs with a strange message from an unknown Arab named Mohammed. These envoys, who had been dispatched from a town in the distant Hejaz called Yathrib — to be renamed Medina, the City of the Prophet — had the audacity to demand that both Heraclius and Khosrau acknowledge Mohammed forthwith as the living apostle of the Lord, Allah. Historical sources give us no idea of how the bizarre injunction was received.

As the third decade of the seventh century drew to a close, the war-weary Heraclius began to reap the fruits of the Byzantine Empire's miraculous redemption. Khosrau had been executed by his son Kavadh II, who sought peace terms, and Heraclius was being hailed as the savior of Christian civilization. Later historians would even honor him as "the first Crusader." On September 14, 629, he arrived triumphantly in liberated Jerusalem to reinstall the True Cross, along with the other relics of faith, and to organize the restoration of the ruined city.

In this glorious moment, fresh word came of the activities of the Arab called Mohammed. Byzantine frontier forces at the town of Mu'tah near the southern tip of the Dead Sea had repelled a surprise attack by a band of three thousand Bedouins on camels and horseback who had come from Medina. Both sides sustained serious losses. Among the Arab dead were the raiders' leaders, Zayd ibn-Harithah, a freed slave and adopted son of the Prophet Mohammed, together with his second in command, Ja'afar at-Tayyar, or "the Flier," the Prophet's cousin and son-in-law. In the words of the English historian Edward Gibbon, the engagement was "the first military action which tried the valor of the Moslems against a foreign enemy."

Fresh from his triumph over the Sassanid Persians, Emperor Heraclius rides in triumph into his capital, Constantinople, bearing the True Cross.

Zayd's troops were a highly disciplined band, entrusted with a vital mission by a ruler with an iron will and a great design. Mohammed ordered them to steal a supply of the famed Mashrafiyeh swords in whose manufacture the town of Mu'tah specialized. Those captured weapons would be used by Mohammed's growing army of converts in a planned campaign to seize the holiest city of pagan Arabia — Mecca. From this coveted base, the Prophet would then launch a *jihad,* or holy war, to impose the faith of the One God, Allah, upon all the idolatrous tribes of Arabia.

Had Allah himself not called upon Mohammed in a vision so many years earlier: "O thou, enwrapped in thy mantle! Arise and warn"? In studying the Holy Book of the Jews, had he not learned that just as Abraham had submitted to the will of God in agreeing to sacrifice his son, Isaac — expressed in the Arabic verb *aslama* — so must the undisciplined Bedouin peoples also submit to Allah if they were to be forged into one nation? Mohammed had been chosen Allah's deputy to convert the Arabs to the code of Islam. The Prophet would speak the message of the Koran — the word of Allah relayed to him by the archangel Gabriel. He would preach it in the *khutbah,* the sermon. He would teach it with the sword, if necessary, first within the land of the Arabs, and then in the "war territory" where Christian and Jewish unbelievers dwelled. For did not the Koran say: "Those that have embraced the faith . . . and fought for the cause of Allah may hope for Allah's mercy"?

In January 630, just four months after Heraclius made his triumphal entry into Jerusalem, Mecca submitted to Mohammed. He smashed the 360 idols in the holy sanctuary, and announced: "Truth hath come, and falsehood hath vanished." He rededicated the Black Stone of the Kaaba to Allah, and declared the city forbidden to infidels.

Early in his ministry, Mohammed could claim only a handful of followers. Yet by 637, only seven years after the Prophet's arrival in Mecca and five years after his death, an Islamic army some 60,000 strong encamped before the gates of Byzantine Jerusalem. The city, hardly recovered from the depredations of the Persians, braced itself for a siege by another enemy — this time one that seemed, to the dazed Christians, to have materialized out of Arabia as though summoned by the devil. In fact, as Patriarch Sophronius urged Christian Jerusalemites to hasten their preparations for this new trial, he preached that their own sins had brought it about.

Heraclius now knew who Mohammed was, for since 634 the Byzantine Empire had been reeling before the unyielding "sword of Allah." Not even the savage Persians had proved such a formidable enemy. The rushing and wheeling of the Arab horse and camel cavalry defied the established Roman rules of set-piece battle, and the likes of such fighting men had never been seen before. The zealous Bedouin troops embraced death as intensely as others clutched to life. In less than two years, the great cities of Byzantine Syria had fallen to them: Bosra, Damascus, Baalbek, Homs, and Aleppo (see map, page 19). In a narrow valley of Yarmuk in northern Palestine, they had virtually annihilated a crack Byzantine army of 25,000 men.

His strength exhausted by unending crises, his resources depleted by two wars, Heraclius prayed in the

great cathedral at Antioch and then abandoned the defense of his southern province. He boarded ship for Constantinople saying: "Farewell, a long farewell to Syria." Antioch fell. There would be no help for Jerusalem.

Even as the Bedouins invested the Holy City, other Arabian armies were bringing Persia and Egypt to heel. But it was Jerusalem that dominated the thoughts of Caliph Omar ibn al-Khattib — the Supreme Commander of the Faithful — a tall, balding man upon whose shoulders the destiny of all Islam rested. That unique city, which crowned the rocky heights of central Palestine, and which was the spiritual magnet of the earlier, monotheistic "Peoples of the Book" — the Jews and Christians — also held a special place in the Koranic teachings of Mohammed. And before his death the Prophet had personally given his friend Omar special instructions concerning the Holy City.

It was only the fiery exhortations of the "honey-tongued" patriarch, Sophronius, that sustained the despairing defenders of Jerusalem against the legions of the "pseudo-Prophet." Oratory was but a temporary antidote, however. After four months, the despondent patriarch appeared on the city's walls to announce that Jerusalem would capitulate, but only on condition that Omar himself receive Sophronius's surrender. Broken by the shame of submission to the infidel, the patriarch took refuge in Omar's acknowledgment that the Steward of the Lord's House was at least the equal of the Supreme Commander of the Faithful. The consolation was momentary — Sophronius would die a comfortless death before the year was out.

The rival leaders met on the Mount of Olives, which rose steeply from the deep Kidron valley east of the city. The Jewish Temple on its huge dais had once stood atop the crest of the ridge immediately opposite. It had been put to the torch by Emperor Titus in A.D. 70, and its rubbled traces had been expunged by the Roman general Hadrian sixty-five years later.

Omar proved to be more charitable than either Titus or Hadrian had been toward the vanquished residents of Jerusalem. He extended to Sophronius a covenant, assuring the Christians of the safety of "their persons, possessions, churches, crosses, their healthy and sick persons, and of all their community. . . . They will not suffer for their religion, nor will any one of them be molested and injured."

The "sternly frugal" Omar, as one early Christian chronicler called him, combined firmness and discipline with deeply human qualities. He owned but a single shirt and mantle, both patched, and he slept on a bed of palm leaves. It is said that he condemned his son to death for excessive drinking and licentiousness. On the other hand, he repented for having had a Bedouin whipped — and ordered his victim to inflict the same punishment on him. He was utterly convinced that the faith of Islam was the one true religion, and he earnestly hoped for conversion among the "Peoples of the Book." Of the Koran, Omar said: "Burn the libraries, for their value is in this book." Yet he was also deeply conscious of Islam's debt to its two parent faiths, and of Jerusalem's universal sacredness as the sanctuary of Jesus and as the holy repository of the traditions of the Israelite forefathers Abraham, Moses, David, and Solomon — all of whom Islam also accepted as prophets.

دو ابین بر ما سے بر ما سیرت دور
این دیوان پنجے کنجہ ہ
بموشرطہ پام
آن پاکیزهنسه
وین شنیده آنجہ و پس کلام
درشب تیرہ نقش مرادنقش پذیر
شدز نقش آن کند نات
گردان از طوق آن گر زبین شاید یافت
طوق زر بین شاید یافت

Omar entered the Holy City astride a white camel. He was piously clothed in a soiled and torn garment of camel's hair. Behind him, in perfect order, trooped some four thousand carefully selected warriors — loyal veterans who could be trusted to obey the caliph's injunctions against looting and abide by the terms of his covenant with the Christians of the conquered city. The grief-stricken Sophronius was given "the humiliating duty" of acting as Omar's guide.

The procession moved to the Church of the Holy Sepulcher, only partially restored since the Persian demolition almost three decades earlier. "I would pray," Omar said to Sophronius, who invited him to spread his prayer rug within the church. But the caliph declined, removing himself instead to the steps outside the eastern doors. There he prostrated himself. "Patriarch," he said upon rising, "dost thou know wherefore I would not pray within the church? You would have lost it, and it would have passed out of your hands, for after I had gone away, the Moslems would have taken it from you, for already they were about to say, 'Here Omar prayed.'" The caliph had keen foresight: a mosque named for him now stands upon the traditional place of his devotions; from its graceful minaret, the *muezzin's* call to prayer mingles with the chants of Christian clerics in the church below.

The time had finally come to carry out Mohammed's injunction. Omar commanded Sophronius to show him the place where King Solomon had erected the first Temple — for the Moslems, like the Jews, held it to be sacred ground.

Some four centuries later, when the Crusaders had regained Jerusalem for Christendom, they too would hold the site of the Temple to be sanctified ground, for to it Jesus had been brought as an infant, had held discourse with the rabbis as a youth, had preached and taught. But in pre-Islamic times, the holy places of the early Christians were located elsewhere. To them the seat of the ancient Temple was accursed ground, for it had been written in the Gospels that Jesus prophesied to the Jews: "Behold, your House shall be left to you forsaken and desolate." And so Sophronius led Omar to what had become a polluted place — the garbage dump of the city. The huge platform of masonry and fill upon which the Temple once stood was now a dung-hill. The Holy of Holies — Mount Moriah, where Abraham had prepared to sacrifice Isaac, and Mount Zion, which King David had acquired from Ornan the Jebusite — was buried in refuse.

Some say that the enraged Omar shouted at the patriarch: "O, ye men of Greece, verily, ye are the people who shall be slain on this dung-heap. . . ." And he commanded Sophronius to begin removing the filth with his own hands. Others relate that Omar lifted up the hem of his garment, filled it with dirt, and cast it into the Kidron valley. His soldiers followed the caliph's example, carrying away the filth in their garments, shields, baskets, and pitchers until the sacred rock appeared. Omar then exclaimed: "By Him in whose hands is my soul! — this is the place described to us by the Apostle of Allah. Let us make this the place for a mosque." Sophronius is then said to have uttered in horror: "Verily, this is the abomination of desolation spoken of by Daniel the Prophet, and it now stands in the Holy Place."

The Prophet had first laid Islam's spiritual claim

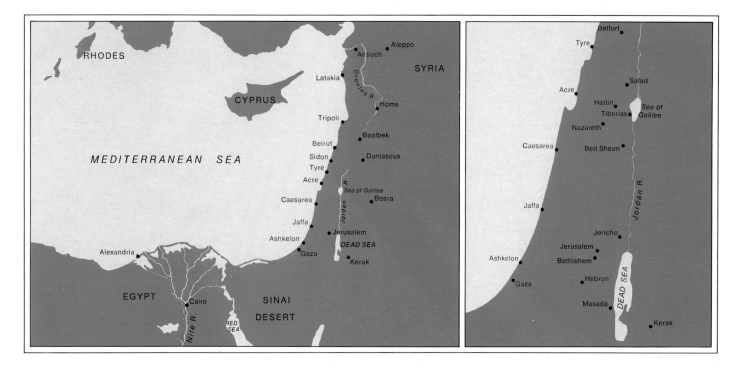

upon Jerusalem years before, in Medina. He had proclaimed the Holy City the first *qibla,* the direction in
which the earliest Moslems, like the Jews, were to
pray. There were two reasons for Mohammed's declaration. First, he hoped to attract Jews in large numbers
to the Islamic creed. The second reason lay in these
words of the Koran:

> Glory be to Him who made His servant (Mohammed)
> go by night . . . to the further Mosque (Jerusalem)
> whose surroundings We have blessed, that We might
> show him some of Our signs. He alone hears all and
> observes all.

This is the basis of the Vision of the Night Journey
to Jerusalem, one of the main threads in the ornate
fabric of Islamic mysticism and legend. The Prophet
himself must have been the first to spellbind his
followers with embellishments of that brief Koranic
allusion to the Holy City. Through the ages the tale
grew more florid. One night in Mecca, a later version
relates, Mohammed mounted his steed al-Burak, "the
Lightning" — a phantasmagorical winged creature with
the face of a woman. His escort was the archangel
Gabriel, the messenger of Allah. Together they sped
through the sky toward Jerusalem, descending briefly
at Mount Sinai and Bethlehem, and finally alighting
upon the Temple's sacred rock. There they were met
by Abraham, Moses, Solomon, Jesus, and other of
Allah's ancient apostles. They prayed together in the
grotto, hollowed beneath the rock, that is known today as the Cave of the Prophets. Then Gabriel guided
the Prophet to the pinnacle of the rock, which the
Arabs call as-Sakhra, where a ladder of golden light
materialized. On this glittering shaft, Mohammed

ascended to the Seventh Heaven. As he was transported
upward, all the delights of Paradise were revealed to
him. The rock attempted to follow, speaking with a
tongue and saying: "O Mohammed, take me along
into the Presence of Allah." As Gabriel fended off the
envious stone, his handprint was etched in its surface.

Brought before Allah, Mohammed received injunctions as to the duties his followers were to perform.
He then descended to as-Sakhra, remounted al-Burak,
and was back in Mecca before the night had waned.

And so, near the sacred rock that was sanctified for
Moslems by the Vision of the Night Journey, Omar
raised his mosque. The sole surviving description of
that structure comes from the annals of Bishop Arcul-
fus, a Christian pilgrim who visited Jerusalem around
670, three decades after the mosque was built:

> In that renowned place where once the Temple had
> been magnificently constructed, placed in the neigh-
> borhood of the wall from the east, the Saracens now
> frequent a four-sided house of prayer, which they have
> built rudely, constructing it by raising boards and
> great beams on some remains of ruins: this house
> can, it is said, hold three thousand men at once.

Rude, perhaps. But the Mosque of Omar ratified the
claim of a third great religion to the Holy City — and
the permanent claim of the city upon the imagination
of the world of Islam. Although Mohammed later
directed that the *qibla,* or focus of prayer, be turned
away from Jerusalem and toward Mecca — which, with
Medina, became the holiest place in Islam — Jerusalem
remained the moon to Mecca and Medina's sun, the
third most sacred Moslem site.

In the half century after Omar's conquest, the Arab

nation consolidated its empire, began to synthesize a new material culture unrivaled in magnificence, and amassed great wealth. And in 687 a successor to the caliphate named Abd al-Malik ibn Marwan replaced Omar's primitive mosque with a building of incomparable magnificence — the Kubbat as-Sakhra, or Dome of the Rock. Its octagonal walls encircled like a diadem the austere jutting crag that the Jews had held to be the center of the earth. Today that eight-sided exterior is sheathed in a radiant mantle of decorated Kutahia tiles and glazed brick rather than the mosaic that originally adorned it. But in all other respects the Dome of the Rock stands today exactly as Abd al-Malik's gifted architects and craftsmen raised it nearly thirteen hundred years ago.

Arab legends relate that the sacred rock once extended twelve miles heavenward, its shadow reaching to Jericho. At its pinnacle was set a ruby so flawless that those who lived in Balkh in far-off Afghanistan could spin their wool at night by its light. Seventy thousand angels stood eternal guard at its base. Here the Ark of Noah rested before the Deluge. Here lay the entrance to Paradise, where the blessed would be segregated from the damned on Judgment Day. Even the holy cities of Mecca and Medina would be transported to Jerusalem on that day, to bear witness to the weighing of the souls of men.

Those who have seen the rising sun burnish the golden dome of the Kubbat as-Sakhra with flaming light count it among the most moving of sights. Ten centuries ago the Arab traveler al-Muqaddasi observed: "At dawn, when the light of the sun first strikes on the cupola, and the drum catches the rays, then is this edifice a marvelous sight to behold, and one such that in all Islam I have never seen its equal."

Set upon the broad raised platform called the Haram Ash-Sharif, the Noble Sanctuary, the Dome of the Rock dominates the walled square mile of medieval Old Jerusalem and comprises one-sixth of its area. The Moslems consider the entire Haram a mosque, and prostrate themselves in prayer everywhere upon it, although the common place of congregation on the Sabbath, Friday, is the basilica-like Further Mosque — al-Aksa — at the southern rim of the platform. Seen from above, the golden sphere of the Dome of the Rock and the silver-domed al-Aksa seem the twin planets of a microcosm — with minor domes, small prayer platforms, ablutions fountains, minarets, green-spired cypresses, and eucalyptus trees clustered like satellites about and between them.

The Haram is cradled within a bowl of hills, its mass like an epicenter of spiritual gravity. The essence of Western spiritual experience, which dates back more than three thousand years, is rooted here, as it is in the ridge lines and slopes of the deep surrounding valleys. Far off to the northwest are the rounded tops of Nabi Samwil, home of the prophet Samuel and summit from which the Crusaders caught their first glimpse of Jerusalem, and Gibeah, royal seat of Saul, first King of Israel. To the northeast is Mount Scopus, with its grove of pines, crowned by the modern university buildings that proclaim the rebirth of Israel.

On the east, separating the Haram from the arid cleft that sheers away steeply to the Wilderness of Judaea and the Dead Sea, is the Mount of Olives. There Jesus spoke to his disciples of the destruction of Jerusalem, and there several churches and a mosque commemorate the Christian tradition of the Ascent to Heaven. The Pilgrim's Way, which ends at the ancient shrines of the Ascension on the summit, winds through the groves of the garden of Gethsemane on the western slope and joins the Via Dolorosa within the walled city. Lying low to the southeast is the Hill of Evil Counsel, where some believe the house of the high priest Caiaphas once stood — and where Peter denied Jesus three times. Lower still, at the foot of the Haram's south retaining wall, lies the seminal Jerusalem of King David, the ten-acre hill of Ophel, which is presently studded with Arab houses and sheep pastures. And to the immediate west of Ophel rises Mount Zion. This is, according to tradition, the site of both the Last Supper and David's Tomb.

The Haram is of the city, but it is also a place apart. The roads of three faiths lead either to the platform itself or to its periphery. Each Friday, a half hour before noon, the *muezzins* climb their spires of stone and wail Sabbath *salaams* to the Moslems of the Old City as the bells of the Christian churches toll in a clash of sound. Stand where the tiny stepped lane called the Aqabat er-Rahbat enters the passage to the Ghawanima Gate at the northern end of the Haram. Arabs in modern dress, Bedouins in peasant robes, and sheikhs in brilliant *jubbahs* and *tarbooshes* answer the *muezzins'* summons: *"Allahu Akhbar!"* — "Allah is most great!" After the ablutions, the removal of shoes, the fixed number of prayer prostrations, and the sermon — a simple service of no more than forty-five minutes — the Arabs depart.

Stand near the same passage a few hours later. New

congregants materialize but do not enter the Haram. Many are clearly from the West — Spain, Italy, Germany, Britain, America. They are taken in hand by Franciscan monks in brown hooded cassocks sashed with white rope, and they are led into the cobbled courtyard of the al-Omariyah public school immediately adjacent to the Haram. At a well-worn stone flanked by two basketball hoops and a tennis net, they begin to pray: *"Miserere nobis Domine. Miserere nobis"* — "Lord have mercy upon us. Have mercy."

These Friday pilgrims are at the first of the Fourteen Stations of the Way of the Cross. Below their feet, under the impacted rubble of earlier Jerusalems, lies the ruins of the great Antonia Fortress, from whose towers Roman centurions once stood watch over the Jewish Temple. Antonia was the praetorium of Pontius Pilate, the spot where Jesus was judged, sentenced to be crucified, and scourged. Following a tradition that is six centuries old — and, in rudimentary form, is considerably older than that — the pilgrims trace the route and symbolically relive the events of Jesus' Passion. Their way leads along the Via Dolorosa — the holiest Christian thoroughfare in the world — through a gauntlet of souvenir shops, jewelry stores, and refreshment stands that attempt to lure the devout from their plane of spiritual reflection. Old Jerusalem has always been a vast jangling incongruity, the setting for a never-ending morality play in which the world of the spirit collides head-on with the world of the flesh.

In its final stages, the Way of the Cross leads upward across the tilted, east-west axis of the Old City to the Church of the Holy Sepulcher, which houses the last five stages of the Passion of Jesus and which has been the goal of the Christian pilgrim's redemptive quest for sixteen centuries. Its bulging gray dome projects upward from among jostling cupolas, spires, minarets, and belfries, as though straining for a glimpse of Heaven. The ancient church and the golden Dome of the Rock roughly one-third of a mile to the east are the spiritual antipodes of the holy war that Christians and Moslems waged here for so long so many years ago. Like the Moslem Dome, the church too shields sacred rock — that of Golgotha, the Place of the Skull, and the traditional tomb of the Resurrection.

The battered stones, piers, and columns of the Church of the Holy Sepulcher bear the wounds of two demolitions, more than fifty earthquakes, and the ceaseless territorial struggles of the six Christian sects that serve as its guardians — Greek Orthodox, Armenian, Roman, Coptic, Syrian, and Abyssinian. Like the church, Jerusalem is a pastiche of conflicting and interacting faiths, creeds, sects, churches, warring traditions, and rival claims. But like the church, Jerusalem also represents continuity and resurrection. The city walls have endured endless besiegers and conquerors — Israelite, Egyptian, Aramaean, Assyrian, Babylonian, Persian, Greek, Roman, Arab, Seljuk, Crusader, Mameluke, Ottoman, British, Jordanian, Israeli — and in the process the crenelated battlements have become a mason's crazy quilt. For example, you will find incorporated in a single Turkish-built wall the reused, shallow-dressed stones of the Maccabaeans; the monumental, deeply framed stones of Herod the Great; the small, smoothly drafted stones of the Byzantines; and the bulging bosses of the Crusaders. Men have rebuilt the ancient city of Jerusalem as obsessively as they

Each Friday, the cry "Allahu Akhbar!" — "Allah is most great!" summons Jerusalem's Moslem population to midday devotions on the Haram Ash-Sharif (right), the raised platform surrounding the Dome. As the Moslems depart, Christian pilgrims converge upon the northwest corner of the Haram. Led by friars in brown cassocks (right, below), these worshipers retrace Jesus' fateful final steps — a route that terminates within the Church of the Holy Sepulcher in the heart of Old Jerusalem. At dusk, the city's Jews gather at the Wailing Wall (below), last remnant of the sacred Temple, to welcome the Sabbath with song and prayer. Thus, within the space of a few hours, the cycle is complete: independently and peaceably, the adherents of three faiths have worshiped at the one site held sacred by all.

have blessed it and demolished it over the centuries.

On this same Friday, as the day begins to wane, leave the Church of the Holy Sepulcher and walk east, back toward the retaining walls of the Haram Ash-Sharif. The worldly Old City is a teeming cosmopolitan supermarket two thousand years old: under ancient arches and vaults, long since abandoned by the buildings they once supported, stands a congeries of suqs displaying caftans, vegetables, and wool. Continue through aromatic clouds of deep-frying *felafel*, coffee, and spices by the sackful; past stalls that defy the rules of modern politics by selling inlaid boxes made in Syria, and soap and candy made in Israel; past traders in shoes and nuts, leather and eggs, sweet pastries, fluttering fowls in cages, exotic cloth, and rugs; past merchants who, perched on rickety wicker stools, whisper the all-purpose, multinational come-on to the bargain hunter: "halloo, halloo." Jostle past Bedouin women in veils, balancing trays of saffron rice and sweet cakes on their heads; past a clopping donkey straining under sacks of United Nations relief flour; past a Coptic priest, Arab porters bent double under heavy bales, very correctly dressed German tourists, a high-ranking *imam* in a *tarboosh* of purple and white, a bearded Ethiopian prelate with black skullcap and frock, ultraorthodox Mea Shearim Jews with broad-brimmed hats and long *peyotim* dangling from their temples. The ear can detect the sounds of clucking roosters, padding camels, clicking heels on terraced passageways, insinuating laughter, the warning of an Arab trying to brake a hurtling pushcart full of mattresses, the sizzling of barbecuing lamb. . . .

The Street of the Chain follows the ancient line of

the thoroughfare that formed the east-west axis of the Roman city. It ends near a vast esplanade carved out of Arab slums by Israeli bulldozers only days after the war of June 1967. Across the plaza rises the western wall of the Haram. The huge crowd gathered before it is highlighted against the huge stone blocks, which reflect the last rays of the setting sun. It is the start of the Jewish Sabbath, and this is the Wailing Wall, the sanctified fragment of the ancient Temple whose loss, some two thousand years ago, Jews still mourn.

But joy is the keynote of the Friday prayer, for men are welcoming the Sabbath as a bride. Some, clad in black frock coats and knee breeches in the medieval manner of the central European ghetto, clutch the ancient prayer shawl, or *tallith*. Others wear the small knitted *yarmulke* and open-neck dress shirt of the assimilated Israeli; still others, the bright leisure wear of the American tourist. The babble of prayer and lusty Hebraic songs of welcome to the Sabbath float into the crystal air. Immediately above is the Haram, Moslem holy ground — and the Dome of the Rock looms silently, almost reprovingly, above those who ignored Mohammed's call. This is the third dimension of the antipodal clash of faith in which Jerusalem has been locked since the days of Omar.

Shema Yisrael, Adonoy Elohenu, Adonoy Echad! — Hear, O Israel, the Lord our God, the Lord is One! All the incongruities and tensions of Jerusalem resolve themselves in the essential harmony of the monotheistic creed — symbolized by this Hebrew prayer — to which the three faiths subscribe. In this uplifting sense of unity in discord lies the perpetual fascination of Jerusalem.

II
The Temples of Israel

In roughly 2000 B.C., when a Semitic nomad the Bible calls Abraham wandered in Canaan with his family and flocks, Jerusalem had not yet acquired its enduring uniqueness. At that time, the city was part of a polytheistic world: a Canaanite people lived within the walls of Ophel and worshiped families of gods — of fertility, of sky and sea and storm, of sun, moon, and soil. Canaanites looked upon the jagged mountaintops as the seats of their divine pantheons, and the great rock of Jerusalem was undoubtedly one of their revered "high places."

In the twentieth and nineteenth centuries B.C., Jerusalem resisted the hegemony of the great pharaohs of Egypt, who demanded obeisance from the petty city-states of Canaan. To tame them, Egyptian priests resorted to magic. They inscribed the names of their pharaohs' enemies on sacred bowls and figurines, then with powerful incantations smashed them as a curse against those "who may rebel, who may plot, who may fight, who may talk of fighting, or who may talk of rebelling — in this entire land." Among those so execrated were two kings of Jerusalem, Yaqar-'Ammu and Setj-'Anu. Those shattered pottery shards thus provide the first written reference to the city. We have no idea what fate befell the two monarchs, but we can safely assume that it was the deities of the sacred rock — perhaps El, the father of the Canaanite pantheon — whose power they invoked to defy the magic of the pharaohs and their great god Amen-Re.

By the fourteenth century B.C. the pharaohs of the New Kingdom were able to command the loyalty of the princes of Canaan without resorting to magic. The imperial Egyptian armies, spearheaded by swift chariots and archers with powerful composite bows, had brought the distant provinces to heel, but administering the new holdings was quite another matter. The petty princelings of the Canaanite city-states were far from secure under Egyptian tutelage, as their cuneiform diplomatic dispatches to the capitals, Thebes and Akhetaten, clearly reveal.

Many Asian Semites — including descendants of the patriarchs who had migrated to Egypt during periods of famine — were by that time held in bondage there, tilling the fields, laboring in the turquoise mines of the desolate Sinai desert, or hauling great stones for the cities and temples that immortalize the masters of the Nile. But others of their kind, land-hungry and undisciplined, had remained behind in Canaan, and they had begun to sweep across the rich land, seizing everything in their path. The vassal rulers of the walled Canaanite towns deluged their masters, Amenhotep III and his son Akhenaten, with frantic reports about these invaders, whom they called Habiru. In a threnody of woe, they complained that the Habiru were seizing the countryside; the Habiru were intriguing with neighboring rivals; the Habiru were at the gates of their cities!

The Prince of Jerusalem, Abdu-Heba, was one of those who moaned most loudly. "The Habiru plunder the lands of the pharaoh," he reported. "If there are archers [here in Jerusalem] this year, the lands of the pharaoh, my lord, will remain [intact]; but if there are no archers [here], the lands of the pharaoh, my lord, will be lost!" In subsequent letters, Abdu-Heba became even more desperate: " . . . There is war against me. I have become like a ship in the midst of the sea."

As this stele attests, warfare has been endemic in Palestine since the third millennium B.C., when Habiru tribesmen first invaded Canaan.

A neighboring ruler had been killed by slaves who were in league with the marauding Habiru, and another, in Shechem to the north, had already surrendered his lands to the Semitic horde.

The similarity between the words Habiru and Hebrew is probably far from coincidental, for among these rampaging Semitic brigands was an advance wave of the Hebrew people, to whom the name came solely to apply. When the hardy second wave, led by Moses and Joshua, arrived late in the thirteenth century B.C. — following an epic march through the wilderness from Egypt that culminated in their historic covenant with the One God at Mount Sinai — at least part of Canaan's hilly central zone was already controlled by their Semitic kinsmen. These people adopted the new religious tradition brought to them by the leaders of the Exodus.

Jerusalem itself resisted the Hebrew onslaught for hundreds of years, remaining in the hands of a Canaanite people whom the Bible calls Jebusites. During the early decades of the Israelite occupation a southern tribe of the Hebrews called Judah assaulted the city, but they failed to hold it. Then, on a day in or about the year 996 B.C., a man of Judah, King David, successfully breached Jerusalem's defenses and fixed its destiny for all time as the epicenter of the monotheistic world.

David was a seasoned soldier and a charismatic leader whose brilliance — like that of modern guerilla chiefs — lay in strategically deploying smaller forces against a superior enemy, in exploiting strength in weakness and weakness in strength. (This is clearly the point of the allegorical tradition of David's battle with Goliath.)

As a favored lieutenant of Saul, the first Israelite king, David bested the powerful Philistines of the Mediterranean coast. When Saul jealously turned against him, David managed to survive in the fringes of the desert as a fugitive bandit chieftain, his exploits capturing the imagination of his own and other tribes.

When the Philistine war turned disastrously against Saul, and his body was hung on the wall of Beit Shean, David's popularity vaulted him to the kingship of Judah, which had its capital at Hebron. This was the political base from which he waged a successful campaign of diplomacy and cunning to supersede Saul's legitimate heirs and win the throne of all Israel.

Endemic contention between the tribes of the north and south plagued Israel at this time. Phoenicians beset the young state from the north, Midianite and Amalekite raiders from the Arabian peninsula to the east. The Jebusites clung stubbornly to their enclave of Jerusalem, which divided Israel's holdings in two. The Philistines applied relentless pressure from the west. Their monopoly on iron-making — and consequently on iron swords, spears, and arrowheads — was the real "Goliath" behind their crucial campaign to expand into the Israelite hill country. David's survival hung on his ability to do what Saul had not been able to do: he succeeded in imposing a fabric of national unity over the Hebrew tribes.

It was David's strategic genius that showed him how that union could be achieved. The answer lay within the gates of Jerusalem. Its capture would remove the Jebusite thorn from Israel's side and secure the lines of communication among the tribes of the north and south. Since the city lay between the two regions and

Combining stealth and daring, David, the youthful king of Judah, wrested Jerusalem from the Jebusites around 996 B.C. The revels that followed his victory are the subject of the twelfth-century illumination at right, which shows David dancing before the Ark of the Covenant as it is borne into the city. In the years that followed, Hebrew artisans were to create a new iconography that fused Canaanite and Israelite imagery. The miniature at left, for example, unites pagan cherubim and the Throne of Mercy, symbol of Yahweh.

belonged to neither, both factions would agree to accept it as their capital. Moreover, as the towering shrine of the holy rock, Jerusalem was more than worthy to serve as the sacred citadel of the Lord Most High, the everlasting King of Israel, who would depose the pagan god El with the help of his servant David. Around such a symbol, all the disparate elements of the national union would cohere; Jerusalem would not only serve as the political capital of Israel, but as its religious hub as well.

But how could the impregnable city, ringed on all sides by natural defenses and imposing battlements, be taken? A direct assault against the ramparts was clearly impossible. David sought a weakness in the powerful defenses, and his intelligence network eventually discovered one. A precipitous water shaft lying within the city descended to the roof of the rock chamber from which the Gihon Spring issued. The shaft allowed the women of the Jebusite city to lower their water jars on ropes and fill them without having to make the arduous climb to and from the spring itself, low in the western flank of the Kidron valley. Here, most probably under cover of night, David's commander, Joab, led a large body of volunteers. Within the cover of the rocky chamber enclosing the spring, torches were lit and ropes were passed to the agile men who spearheaded the climb up the shaft and into the unsuspecting city.

Before the alarm could be spread, Joab's men had penetrated the defenses, reduced key Jebusite strongpoints along the walls, and opened the eastern gates to David's main forces, which crouched silently outside. Jerusalem, which had resisted conquest for centuries, surrendered virtually intact.

Amid scenes of rejoicing, the Ark of the Covenant — which held the holiest relics of the Israelites, the tablets of the Ten Commandments brought by Moses from Mount Sinai — was borne to its new resting place, Jerusalem, in a lurching ox-drawn cart preceded by a huge troupe of musicians. Melodies of gladness and praise were sounded on horns, harps, and lyres — a din, augmented by the throbbing rhythms of tambourines, castanets, and cymbals, that reached to the heavens and echoed and reechoed from the hills. Next in the procession came the dancers, King David among them, leaping wildly to the shouts of the ecstatic crowds that lined the route to the city.

This was the very Ark, of acacia wood and beaten gold, that the Lord had commanded Moses to build in the desert. Borne on its poles by the priestly clans of the tribe of Levi, it had preceded Joshua's Israelites from the plains of Moab to the very walls of Jericho. It had led the Israelites into battle against the Philistines, only to be captured at the battle of Aphek and held for a time while Israel's fortunes were at their lowest ebb.

Now that the wandering nation had finally carved a secure place for itself in Canaan, the portable Ark — symbolic of a unique bond between the children of Israel and their ever-present God — had come to the end of a journey that had begun at Mount Sinai nearly three hundred years earlier. Before the Ark, David sacrificed an ox and a fatling and led his people in a huge feast of thanksgiving. Jerusalem would be sanctified above all cities by the Ark's presence — and its tablets defining the moral relationship among men and between man and God would ultimately become the basis of the Judeo-Christian ethic.

But how would the Ark be housed? David had provided it with a city, but not a permanent dwelling. He was far too occupied enlarging Israel's holdings and securing its borders to be concerned about great public works; that task would fall to a man of peace who had the time and energy for such things as erecting a holy temple. But even as he waged war, David began making preparations for the House of God that his son and successor, Solomon, would construct. From his vanquished enemies, David collected vast riches in spoils and tribute: stores of gold, silver, and bronze, and iron for nails and clamps. From his Phoenician allies he began to obtain the highly prized cedar wood of the forests of Lebanon. Conquered Jebusites were pressed into service cutting large quantities of honey-pale limestone from the city's virtually inexhaustible quarries. Before David's death, there remained but two things for him to do: he charged Solomon with the task of building the Temple, and he purchased the land surrounding the sacred rock from Ornan the Jebusite — who had used it as a threshing floor — for fifty shekels of silver. "Here," David said, "shall be the house of the Lord God."

Solomon, who came to power around 970 B.C., was the perfect complement to his father. David had been preeminent in the field of battle; Solomon was unsurpassed as an administrator, builder, diplomat, and commercial entrepreneur, and he led Israel into its all-too-brief golden age.

Spiritually, the Israelites' conception of the divine order was more advanced than that of the polytheistic peoples of the region; but their material culture lagged far behind. Solomon's people were still shackled to the spartan, seminomadic ways of the desert, pastureland, and fields of war from which they had so recently come. To train his subjects in the pursuits of peace and the sophisticated ways of the city, Solomon turned to Israel's ally, King Hiram of Phoenicia, for technical assistance. Hiram's worldly artisans, craftsmen, architects, and engineers would not only teach the Israelites to draft stone, shape silver and gold, cut precious stones, cast bronze, dye and weave wool and linen, work iron and wood, carve ivory, and design fortifications, public buildings, and palaces, they would also help Solomon to raise his Temple. In exchange for shipments of grain, olive oil, and wine from Israel, Hiram placed the skill of his Tyrians at Solomon's disposal, and shipped additional supplies of timber by sea to Jaffa.

The design of the holy sanctuary was drawn from the great temples built by the Canaanites and Phoenicians to house the graven images of their divine pantheon: El, the father; Baal, god of nature, sun, and storm; Anath, his sister, goddess of war; and Astarte, goddess of fertility or increase in the field, flock, and family. But the concept behind the Temple of Jerusalem was unlike any other. Its God was indivisible, ruling all things of this world and that which lay above and beneath. No mere physical image could adequately represent him; idols were abominations. Moreover, unlike the pagan sanctuaries or high places, the Temple would serve as the house of the Word of the Lord, not of the Deity himself. For the One God was infinitely great and could not be housed in any man-made dwelling. The Temple would merely serve as the symbol of his all-pervading presence. As Solomon said upon its dedication: "Behold, heaven and earth cannot contain

Thee; how much less this house which I have built?"

Completed around 950 B.C., the "House of Israel" was the crowning achievement of Solomon's reign. It was built on a platform of ashlars finely drafted by Phoenician masons. The rectangular building stood forty-five feet high, ninety feet long, and thirty feet wide. It fronted upon a large courtyard, and like other Semitic temples it faced east toward the rising sun. The Temple was flanked by three-story-high side chambers that probably contained rooms for the treasury, the holy vessels and implements, the priestly robes, the vessels for storing the pure beaten olive oil that was used in the holy lamps, and the priceless spices burned as incense.

Like its Semitic prototypes, the building was divided into three main sections. First was the *ulam,* or vestibule, which corresponds to the porch of present-day churches. Beyond was the *hekal,* a sixty-foot-long nave dimly illuminated by light streaming through a series of narrow windows just below the ceiling and richly scented by the floors of cypress and the cedar that lined its lofty walls. At the far western end of the nave lay the innermost shrine, the *debir* or Holy of Holies. It was a perfect windowless cube, thirty feet on each side and lighted by a single oil lamp. Only the high priest was allowed to enter this space of awe and silence — the symbolic throne of the Invisible Presence — and he entered once a year, on the solemn Day of Atonement. Here in flickering shadow stood the two sentinels, winged sphinxes made of olive wood inlaid with gold. The cherubim, as they were known, stood fifteen feet high. Beneath their delicately carved outspread wings lay the Ark with its tablets of the Law.

In the courtyard of the Temple stood an immense basin of cast bronze, seven and a half feet high and roughly fifteen feet in diameter, called the molten sea. Scholars calculate that the basin, which was most probably used by priests for lustrations, held ten thousand gallons of water and weighed some thirty tons. Near it stood the great horned altar for burned sacrifice. That fifteen-foot-high structure was built in a series of recessed stages, much like the enormous tower-temples, or ziggurats, of the Babylonians, and it was probably modeled on them. Around the altar the rites of the Temple revolved.

Upon it was performed the mysterious and complicated ritual of sacrifice to God — a ritual traceable to dimmest antiquity and man's primordial desire to propitiate the angry spirits of a hostile world. Some pagan sects believed that their gods would be satisfied with nothing less than the offering of human life. To the Israelites, however, human sacrifice was an abomination of a particularly loathsome order. In their usage, the sacrificial offering came to signify expiation and denial — a symbolic obligation which reminded man that in the midst of his material bounty he was also a creature of the spirit.

Before the great altar Israelites gathered to pray at the twice-daily offering of a year-old lamb. Men brought a measure of barley to celebrate the beginning of the spring yield, and the first fruits of field and orchard to mark the rich harvest of summer. They gathered about the altar in vast numbers at Passover for their portion of the paschal lamb, which commemorated release from bondage in Egypt. The humble came to offer doves or pigeons in atonement or grati-

*Their graceful movements reduced to mere
schemata, dancers and choristers pinwheel
about King David in this Byzantine manuscript
illumination. The enthroned monarch's son
Solomon appears at his side. Above them looms the
benign countenance of the Hebrew god, Yahweh.*

tude; the well-to-do, bulls "without blemish," goats, rams, or costly incense.

The Temple, with its restrained magnificence, was part of a royal precinct that included Solomon's lavish palace complex: the House of the Forest of Lebanon, named in celebration of the source of the timber of Phoenicia; the Hall of Pillars; the Hall of the Throne; and the Hall of Judgment, where Solomon administered justice. All were clustered on walled terraces around the shelf of high rock immediately north of the City of David. The Throne of God and its royal enclosure rose as a crown above Jerusalem.

As they worked in the fields, wove garments, or journeyed on lonely roads to distant places, men turned in the direction of the Temple to pray. So embedded did this place become in the Hebrew consciousness that long after the Temple and Solomon's kingdom lay in ruins and its people were scattered throughout the world they continued to orient their synagogues in the direction of Jerusalem with its Sanctuary of the Lord, focusing upon it their aspirations and yearnings. The Temple site was a folk magnet whose mystical power defies both explanation and expression.

The holy rock stood at the center of many a temporal crisis as well. With the death of Solomon, the tenuous union created by his father dissolved as the northern tribes flocked to the rebel Jeroboam, who usurped the name Israel for his kingdom. Jerusalem remained the capital of the southern kingdom called Judah. Jeroboam, who saw the Temple as a deadly rival, attempted to undermine its prestige by establishing rival sanctuaries with calves of gold at Bethel and Dan. But as secession, intrigues, and invasions sapped the strength of the two states, the Temple and its spiritual defenders grew in power and authority, overshadowing the temporal authorities of both Israel and Judah.

The periods of peace were few. The kings of Judah were forced to strip the Temple of its votive treasures to appease the appetites of conqueror after conqueror seeking plunder and tribute. In 721 B.C., after a three-year siege of the northern capital of Samaria, Sargon II of Assyria liquidated Israel and turned it into an Assyrian province. Tiny Judah was all that remained of the empire of David and Solomon.

In 587 B.C., Nebuchadnezzar of Babylon, the great superpower of the age, fell heavily upon hapless Judah. He invested Jerusalem for nearly two years, and when it was conquered, the life of the Kingdom of Judah died with it. Famine and illness decimated the population; the Temple was sacked, burned, and razed to the ground; and the sacred vessels and implements were carried off to Babylon. They were followed by thousands upon thousands of captive citizens — princes, soldiers, priests, merchants, craftsmen, and smiths. In one of the earliest recorded examples of forcible mass resettlement, the wrathful Nebuchadnezzar had chosen to expunge an entire nation and its people. His bold plan was staggeringly successful — for all intents and purposes, Jerusalem and Judah had ceased to exist.

The citizens of Judah spent their Babylonian exile in endless bereavement for the desolation of their Temple and their city, "the perfection of beauty, the joy of all the earth." By the slowly moving waters of the broad Euphrates, their laments were lifted heavenward, their tears carried to the sea. The Book of Lamentations preserves their grief:

The Lord has scorned his altar,
    disowned his sanctuary . . .
What can I say for you, to what compare you,
    O daughter of Jerusalem?
What can I liken to you, that I may comfort you,
    O virgin daughter of Zion?
For vast as the sea is your ruin;
    Who can restore you?

Less than half a century later, in 539 B.C., there came a miraculous deliverance. Cyrus of Persia toppled the empire of Babylonia and began to erect his own dominion. Cyrus won the gratitude and loyalty of Nebuchadnezzar's victims by releasing all the captive minorities. In his own words, he "returned (to them) their habitations and resettled . . . all the gods . . . in their sacred cities." The first body of Jewish returnees, under Zerubbabel, a descendant of the House of David, entered Jerusalem and found a wasteland. The population of all Judah, now the Persian province of Yehud, was no more than 20,000.

Zerubbabel's first task was to ferret for shelter and sustenance amid the ruins; his second, to rebuild the shattered Temple. The work began in 520 B.C. with the blessings of Darius I, who allotted moneys from the royal purse toward its construction and returned the sacred regalia looted by Nebuchadnezzar. But the relics of the desert covenant, the Ark and the tablets of Moses, had been lost forever, their place in the *debir* marked henceforth by a simple slab of stone, their words enshrined on parchment in the Torah, or Scroll of the Law.

The new sanctuary rose upon a platform 170 feet wide and more than 500 feet long, but biblical meas-

urements of the Temple itself are deficient. Moreover, the rebuilt Temple would never bear comparison with its predecessor, for the first Temple had been built under Solomon, when "silver was as common as stone in Jerusalem." These were hard times, and the shouts of joy from some who watched the men at work were mingled with the weeping of the elders who had seen the splendor of Solomon's matchless Temple with their own eyes. Yet nothing was stinted at the feast that inaugurated the new Temple in 515 B.C. Twelve he-goats — one for each of the tribes of Israel — plus one hundred bulls, two hundred rams, and four hundred lambs were offered upon the altar.

The magnet of the Jews had been restored — humble though it might now seem — and for two centuries the citizens also restored the land, under the protection of the Achaemenids. But the Persian empire foundered in its wars with Greece, and by 332 B.C. western Asia capitulated to a new conqueror, the megalomanic Alexander the Great. When the Macedonian died suddenly in 323, in the midst of creating a world empire, Alexander's generals carved up his vast holdings. The Ptolemies ruled Egypt, but the rival line of Seleucus, who ruled Syria, forcibly challenged their inheritance of Palestine and won.

The Seleucid king Antiochus IV, who styled himself Epiphanes, or "God-manifest," viewed the unhellenized Jews with disdain. Given over to execrable judgment and fits of temper prompted in part by the growing challenge of Rome, Antiochus decided that the Jews must be made to conform to the more enlightened manners and mores of the Greek world. They must abandon such alien customs as circumcision and

their puritanical codes of cleanliness and diet. They must accept his divinity, and also submit to the worship of Olympian Zeus. The Jews resisted, and in 169 Antiochus marched on Jerusalem to enforce his edicts. He pillaged the Holy Temple and carried off its vessels and many of its treasures. Two years later, his officers defiled the sanctuary again, this time erecting an image of Zeus and a pagan altar, upon which they sacrificed swine. The Scroll of the Law was torn up and burned. This was the ultimate incitement, and the Jews' reaction was swift and violent. They arose in rebellion under the leadership of an aged priest named Mattathias the Hasmonaean and his five sons, known as the Maccabees. In 164, three years to the very day on which the profanation had occurred, the Maccabees drove the Seleucids from the Temple compound. It was cleansed, purified, and rededicated — to the music of the harp, lute, and cymbal — in a display of unrestrained celebration reminiscent of David's procession into the Holy City with the Ark some eight hundred years earlier.

The profound shame of Antiochus's defilement hardened the resolve of the shaken Jews to prevent a similar experience in the future. And so the Maccabaean rulers determined that the Temple must also become a fortress. The holy site was equipped with stout walls and strong towers, and an immense dry moat 60 feet deep and 250 feet broad was dug on its vulnerable northern side. It might have been thought impassable, but the vain and ambitious Pompey and his Roman legions proved otherwise. Exploiting political strife in Judaea, Pompey advanced on Jerusalem from Syria in 63 B.C.

Noting that the Temple was bounded by natural ravines on three sides, he ordered his troops to begin filling in the great moat. When the immense earthworks were finished, siege engines were rolled up to batter and reduce the Temple's northern wall. Jewish defenders harried the enemy with clouds of arrows and showers of stones from the towers above, and it took Pompey three months to effect a breach. Finally, a tower and part of the wall were toppled. As the Roman soldiers swarmed onto the broad expanse of the Temple court, the zealous priests continued to pray and sacrifice at the great altar, pouring libations and offering incense. They were slaughtered where they stood, together with many citizens. In wild flight from the Roman soldiers, other defenders leaped from the high pinnacle of the Temple platform on the east to their deaths in the Kidron valley below. Henceforth, it was not only to God but to the eagle of imperial Rome that Judaea would pay tribute.

Despite the carnage, Jerusalem was entering another golden age. Its glitter was deceptive, however, for beyond it lay the Apocalypse. Both the renaissance and the catastrophe stemmed from the meeting of the Hellenized Roman and the Oriental Jew. The one, worldly and heathen; the other, singularly independent and proud of a coherent religious tradition that made him unique in the civilized world. Roman materialism could never be married to abstract Judaism, but Herod the Great, a complex product of both worlds, saw himself as the matchmaker. Rarely has history known a more ebullient and tragic figure.

Herod's father, Antipater, a fiery Idumaean Arab whose ancestors had been forcibly converted to Judaism, was readily adaptable to Roman uses. Antipater became a trusted lieutenant of Pompey; then, after his assassination, of Julius Caesar and Mark Antony, who conferred Roman citizenship upon him. From his Romanized father, Herod learned the art of survival in the hazardous arena of Roman politics. Under Mark Antony's patronage he was made governor of Galilee, and in 39 B.C. he was confirmed by the Roman senate as King of the Jews, with Antony his sponsor.

When civil war broke out between Antony and Octavian, Herod was ready to take to the field for his patron. But following Antony's disastrous defeat at Actium in 31 B.C., Herod cleverly sped to Rhodes to pledge his loyalty to Octavian, who was to become Emperor Augustus. In doing so Herod acquired the support of an appreciative new suzerain and the reward of more lands in the bargain.

In all things—from cruelty to magnanimity—Herod was larger than life. Cursed by the paranoia of power to distrust those nearest him, he had three sons, his beloved wife, Mariamne, his mother-in-law, and his brother-in-law assassinated or executed. Above all things, Herod wanted acceptance — both by the Romans, whose favor he so desperately curried, and by the Jews, who despised him for his cruelties and posturings to the pagan occupier. And so he raised great buildings to win the awe, if not the love, of Roman and Jew alike. He built with a passion unmatched in Palestine since Solomon's time, a thousand years before his own. He raised huge temples and statues in the name and image of Augustus, and he created one of the most magnificent ports in the

ancient Near East, Caesarea, in honor of the emperor.

On the skyline of Jerusalem, Herod wrought his greatest wonders — a theater, a circus, a hippodrome, massive towers (one 135 feet high), and a great palace and citadel west of the Temple compound. But it was for the Temple itself that he reserved his greatest efforts. Although the Jews of Judaea and those scattered from Alexandria to Delos faithfully dispatched tithes to its treasury, it had never attained the legendary grandeur of Solomon's Temple. Could the Jews long withhold their affection from the monarch who would restore, even surpass that grandeur, Herod wondered? He summoned the high priest and the royal architect. He would have a temple of unrivaled excellence on the sacred site, one that would not in any way offend tradition or depart from the biblical ordinances. Despite these limitations, the edifice must be seen by Jew and Gentile alike as one of the wonders of the world. Indeed, the rabbis of Herod's time, who would scarcely go out of their way to speak kindly of the king, wrote of his creation: "He who has not set eyes upon the structure of Herod has not seen a structure of beauty in all his life."

Ten thousand workmen were recruited, and a thousand priests were trained as stonemasons to work on those portions of the shrine that were not to be handled by the unordained. Construction began in 20 B.C., the seventeenth year of Herod's reign. Labor gangs first set about extending the great stone platform on which the Temple stood. The rocky shelf was leveled on the north, and the ravines to the west and south were buried under thousands of tons of fill. The massive podium rested on great vaults and piers of quarried

stone, and the mammoth retaining walls for the raised court were anchored firmly in the bedrock. Course upon course, the retaining walls rose. Each row was, on an average, three feet high, and some of the larger stones extended to a length of as much as forty feet. At the southeast angle, a tower rose 211 feet above the undulating bedrock of the Kidron valley. This was the "pinnacle" of the Temple, the spot from which Jesus' brother James would be cast down and killed in A.D. 62. It was so high, the rabbis said, that from its parapet "an Arab with a spear looked like a flax worm."

In total area, the podium covered a million square feet, three times larger than the esplanade of the Acropolis in Athens. And as the first-century Jewish historian Flavius Josephus observed, "The whole area was paved with stones of every kind and color." Eight gates pierced the outer bulwark, opening onto the immense plaza from the cardinal points of the compass. Most worshipers used the double complex of entrances and exits on the south, named in honor of the prophetess Huldah, which fronted onto the City of David and were approached by long ramps. On the west, two of the gates opened onto bridges leading to the Upper City — the massive royal stoa reserved for the king, and another for the priests.

Great cloisters ringed the perimeter of the platform. On the north, east, and west, these porches or colonnades were covered by paneled cedar ceilings supported on double rows of white marble columns thirty-seven and a half feet high. Along the southern rim the colonnade widened to encompass the magnificent Royal Porch, with its 162 Corinthian columns in four stately rows.

Now fragmented and timeworn, the inscription at left once enjoined all Gentiles from entering the Temple precincts. Only Jews could gain access to the inner courtyards, and only males could offer sacrifices in the Court of the Israelites. In Roman times the alabaster columns and gold lintels of the Temple shared the skyline with the squat watchtowers of Herod's Antonia Fortress — as the archaeologically faithful and remarkably realistic scale-model below indicates. A portion of Antonia still stands, but most of Herod's Upper City lies beneath the compacted rubble of subsequent settlements. Recent excavations (right) have exposed a number of Herodian structures that once stood just north of the Zion Gate (visible at rear).

These porches formed the outer boundary of the so-called Court of the Gentiles, the teeming crossroads of Jerusalem. There elders gathered to exchange gossip and take the sun, money changers haggled with pilgrims from abroad, and merchants hawked pigeons, sheep, and oxen for the sacrifice. Within this outer court — fenced on four sides by a low balustrade, fourteen steps, and a stone wall breached by ten gates of silver and gold — was the terrace known as the Sacred Precincts. Only Jews could pass into this holy sanctum. Set into the balustrade were stone plaques in Hebrew, Greek, and Latin bearing the proscription: "No Gentile shall enter the fence and barrier around the Holy Place. Whosoever is caught therein will be responsible for his own subsequent death."

The inner sanctum itself was cordoned into three parts. Men and women passing through the great gate of Corinthian bronze, the gift of an Alexandrian Jew named Nicanor, entered the Court of Women. Only males were permitted to ascend the fifteen steps to the graven door of silver and gold that led into the Court of the Israelites. There they offered sacrifices and watched the ceremonies in the Court of Priests, where the great horned altar of unhewn stones stood — perhaps above the sacred rock itself. To the ecstatic cacophony of praying and singing and the blowing of trumpets, beasts tethered to golden rings were slaughtered and roasted over flaming logs of fig, walnut, or pine wood. The blood ran into runnels at the base of the altar and flowed through conduits to the Kidron valley below.

The terraced dais erupted in an architectural crescendo. Looming above the splendid spectacle was the sanctuary itself, a Hellenistic masterpiece with a façade of white marble 150 feet square and bordered by a magnificent lintel of golden grapevines. Two stately fluted columns flanked its great doorway, which was screened by a Babylonian tapestry of blue, scarlet, and purple worked with "the whole vista of the heavens." The capitals were of gold, as were the spikes that punctuated the parapet to discourage roosting birds. According to Josephus:

[The sanctuary was] overlaid all around with stout plates of gold. In the first rays of the sun it reflected so fierce a blaze of fire that those who endeavored to look at it were forced to turn away as if they had looked straight at the sun. To strangers as they approached it seemed in the distance like a mountain covered with snow; for any part not covered with gold was dazzling white.

Drawn to this spectacular setting, thousands upon thousands of pilgrims swelled the city's normal population of 150,000 on the High Holy Days. They streamed from other parts of Judaea as well as from Syria, Phoenicia, Greece, Egypt, Cyprus, and Cyrenaica for Passover in the spring; the Pentecost, or celebration of the summer harvest; the Feast of Booths, a time of thanksgiving for the autumn yield; and Yom Kippur, the Day of Atonement.

Looking down upon the crowds from the four high turrets of the Antonia fortress, built by Herod at the northwest angle of the Temple compound and named for Mark Antony, were the ever-present Roman sentries. At festival times the Roman infantry unit garrisoned at Antonia was placed on alert, for the teeming plaza of the Temple was a potential flash point for sedition and revolt. It was one such holiday vigil that brought the procurator Pontius Pilate from the Roman capital at Caesarea to Jerusalem — for the Passover during which Jesus was crucified.

Many of the threads of Jesus' life, his ministry, and his death lie in the rich fabric of the Temple and its environs. After his birth, Mary and Joseph brought Jesus to the Temple to "present him to the Lord" and to offer sacrifice. It was after a Passover pilgrimage that the twelve-year-old Jesus was found by his anxious parents in disputation with the religious teachers. On yet another Passover pilgrimage, he violently assailed the merchants and money changers in the Court of the Gentiles. On the eastern porch, or Portico of Solomon, he was nearly stoned and arrested as he ministered to the crowd. On the high southeastern "pinnacle," one part of his Temptation occurred. The Temple was the house that he threatened to destroy, and the fortress of Antonia may well have been the place where he was judged by Pilate.

Jesus is said to have prophesied: "Do you see these great buildings? There will not be left here one stone upon another, that will not be thrown down." Many, the Essene authors of the Dead Sea Scrolls among them, were predicting that this chaotic age marked the end of days. Herod's death in 4 B.C. had been followed by a series of revolts among the Jews, culminating in the crucifixion of two thousand of the agitators by the Romans. Archelaus marked his succession to the rule of Judaea by massacring three thousand Passover pilgrims in the Temple court. There were violent protests — against heavy-handed and corrupt procurators, repressive taxes, and Roman persecutions. Each was

followed by a new wave of slaughter. In one such incident at the Temple, Josephus relates that a Roman soldier "pulled up his garment and bent over indecently, turning his backside toward the Jews and making a noise as indecent as his attitude." Furious worshipers threw fusillades of stones at the troops; reinforcements rushed to the colonnades; and in the panic thousands of Jews were crushed to death.

Men whose culture was founded upon faith found themselves adrift, convinced that the Lord had abandoned them. Despair turned to anger, and anger flashed into revolt. It was a particularly inept and callous procurator named Gessius Florus who touched off the final catastrophe. In A.D. 66 he seized a large amount of money from the treasury of the Temple, and his troops butchered a number of outraged Jews. In August of that year a band of Zealots ambushed the Roman garrison at the Dead Sea fortress of Masada, which had originally been built as a royal redoubt by Herod, and seized weapons from the armory. Simultaneously, the populace of Jerusalem rose up against the legionaries, bottling them up in Antonia and Herod's palace. The outnumbered Romans eventually surrendered; meanwhile, the Syrians of Caesarea massacred virtually the entire Jewish community of 20,000 — much to the delight of Florus.

Fury swept the countryside, which quickly followed Jerusalem's example and threw off the Roman yoke. The governor of Syria, Cestius Gallus, marched on Jerusalem from Antioch to restore order. After a siege, during which the Temple area nearly fell to the enemy, Cestius unaccountably called for a general withdrawal. The retreat turned into a disaster when his column was

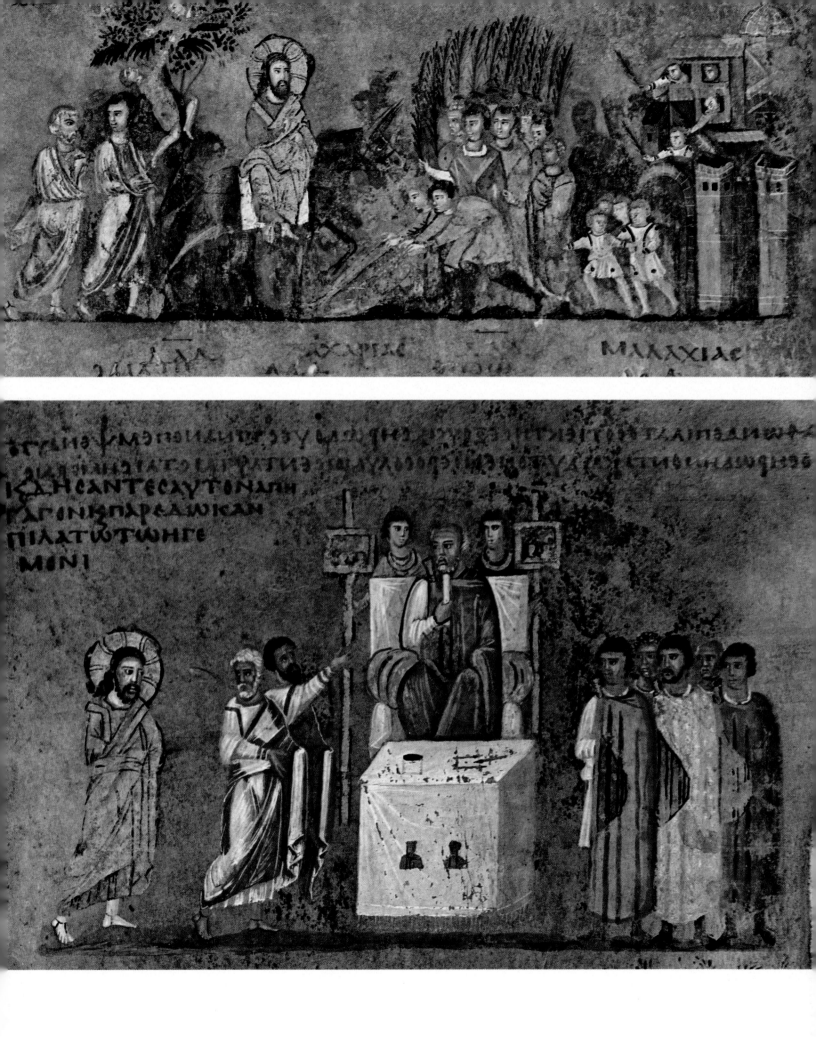

ΑΛΛ
ΖΑΧΑΡΙ
ΜΑΛΑΧΙΑC

ΙΔΗCΑΝΤΕCΑΥΤΟΝ ΑΛΛ
ΓΑΓΟΝΚΑΠΑΡΕΔΩΚΑΝ
ΠΙΛΑΤΩΤΩΝΓΕ
ΜΟΝΙ

ambushed at the Beth-Horon pass northwest of Jerusalem, permitting large quantities of war matériel to fall into the hands of the rebels.

But Jewish successes and independence were to be short-lived, for imperial Rome had been badly stung. Its resources were limitless, and the needs of colonial discipline called for savage retribution against those who dared defy it. An alarmed Nero, who sat upon a shaky throne, called one of his temporarily retired generals back to duty to restore order in Palestine. Vespasian, the emperor's aging field commander, was a ruthless and canny veteran who had fought successfully for the empire in Germany and Britain. After raising an army, he systematically swept through Galilee. Moving first southward, then eastward — his legions meeting fanatical resistance all the way — Vespasian methodically destroyed each village, town, and city in his path. Jerusalem, the last major objective, was saved when civil war broke out in Rome, distracting Vespasian with nothing less than the prospect of the imperial throne, to which his forces in the east were to elevate him. Late in A.D. 69 the Roman senate affirmed Vespasian as "monarch of the world" — and the task of reducing the capital of the Jews fell upon the new emperor's son Titus.

Early in the spring of 70, Titus decamped from Caesarea on the coast and marched eastward toward Jerusalem with four full legions and auxiliaries — spearmen, archers, cavalry, infantry, and engineers. Marching six abreast, Titus's troops easily overwhelmed the handful of irregulars, citizen-soldiers, and hardened Zealot insurgents who massed against them. No sooner had Titus arrived before the city and begun a recon-

naissance than a band of Jews poured from one of the gates, cut through his personal cavalry, and fell upon him. Alone, Titus cut his way through the attackers and made his way safely to camp.

Jerusalem was defended by three walls. One girdled the Lower City (the original City of David) and the Upper City. A second bracketed an area, immediately to the northwest of the Temple, that contained wool shops, the cloth market, and the quarter of the blacksmiths. A third rampart, begun by Agrippa I but never finished, contained the sprawling northern suburb of Bethesda.

Titus's legions encamped north and west of the city. With battering rams pounding and siege towers showering volleys of suppressing fire upon the defenders, the Romans crashed through the outer wall at a point north of Herod's Citadel. Soon thereafter, the second wall was breached and the northwest quarter of the city was taken against fierce resistance. Platforms for the siege engines then began to rise before the walls of Antonia and the Upper City.

By this time the defenders were running out of food, and while raiders sallied from the gates of the first wall to disrupt Titus's assault preparations, other Jews slipped through Roman lines to scavenge for wild plants and herbs. Many were caught. Josephus, an eyewitness to the siege, records that it was not safe for Titus "to let men captured by force go free, and to guard such a host of prisoners would tie up a great proportion of his troops. . . . The soldiers themselves through rage and bitterness nailed up their victims in various attitudes as a grim joke, till owing to the vast numbers there was no room for the crosses, and no

crosses for the bodies." Jerusalemites observing these
horrors from the walls were under no delusions as to
what defeat would mean.

From within the city, desperate defenders burrowed
tunnels beneath the two siege platforms near Antonia,
propping them up with wood soaked in pitch. When
the props were set afire, the tunnels tumbled, under-
mining the platforms — which collapsed with a roar
and were consumed by the flames. Two days later, the
other two platforms were similarly dispatched by Jews
who audaciously sprang from the gates with burning
brands and raced into the midst of the surprised
Romans.

In his mounting desperation Titus called a council
of war. The siege would have to be protracted, for
wood was so scarce that it was impossible to erect new
platforms speedily. The Jews would have to be further
demoralized by starvation while foraging teams located
the timber. Titus ordered that a circumvallation wall
be built around the entire city to keep supplies from
reaching the inhabitants. Its extent, four and a half
miles in circumference, gives some idea of the scale of
the Roman effort. The scope of the suffering and
devastation was equally vast. Josephus records that "in-
numerable corpses piled up all over the city," emitting
a "pestilential stench." Weary and starving, the defenders "devoured belts and shoes, and stripped off the
leather from their shields and chewed it. Some tried
to live on scraps of old hay. . . ."

It took the better part of a month for timber to be
collected, but in time four new towers were erected
along the walls of Antonia, where Titus had chosen to
concentrate his final effort. Rocking and levering the

walls with rams and crowbars, the Romans finally
crashed into the fortress, and from there into the
Temple's outer court. The last line of defense for the
Jews would be the Temple itself. Its fate was sealed,
both by the events and by circumstances, for were the
besiegers to let the Temple stand, it would serve as a
rallying point for rebellious Jews throughout the
Roman world.

Six hundred and fifty-seven years to the day on which
the Babylonians had plundered and razed the first
Temple, its successor fell. The Jewish Temple would
never rise again. On Titus's command the Romans
laid bonfires against its gates. The woodwork beneath
the gold and silver plates caught fire, and the precious
metals melted and ran like water. Their fury whetted
by the long siege, Roman soldiers with burning fire-
brands rushed in and set the sanctuary itself ablaze.
Soldiers, priests, women, children, and old men cower-
ing behind the walls of the Sacred Precincts and within
the colonnades were butchered as the flames roared
through the Temple. According to Josephus:

> The entire city seemed to be on fire, while as for the
> noise, nothing could be imagined more shattering or
> more horrifying. There was the war-cry of the Roman
> legions as they converged; the yells of the partisans
> encircled with fire and sword; the panic flight into
> the arms of the enemy of the people cut off above,
> their shrieks as the end approached. . . . Many who
> were wasted with hunger and beyond speech, when
> they saw the sanctuary in flames, found strength to
> moan and wail. Back from Peraea and the mountains
> round about came the echo in a thunderous bass.

The Lower City went up in flames. The Upper City,

where the defenders made a final stand, was pounded to rubble. Thousands upon thousands of Jews perished in battle or from hunger and disease. Of those who survived, some were put to the sword and some — the attractive and hardy young — were shipped to Rome to grace the victory procession. The rest were either sold into slavery or dispatched to amphitheaters throughout the provinces to be dismembered by gladiators, by each other, or by wild animals for the amusement of the crowds.

The victory pageant in Rome was memorialized by artists and historians. The captives and the spoils of the Temple — including the great, golden, seven-branched menorah and the Scroll of the Law — were paraded before the enormous crowds. A depiction of the scene is visible today on the triumphal arch of Titus in Rome. To commemorate the event, Vespasian and Titus struck coins showing a desolate woman slumped in dejection beneath a palm tree. The coin was pointedly inscribed: *Judaea Capta.*

The remains of the gutted Temple were pulled down, its great stones and rubble hurled from the parapet of the platform by the warriors who camped on the ruins. Only the mammoth blocks of the retaining wall buttressing the western side of the Temple platform were left intact. To these battered stones, Jews in later centuries came to pour out their anguish and grief over a loss that would never be fully assuaged — and over greater holocausts to come. This lone remnant of the second Temple was to become the Wailing Wall.

Incredibly, Jewish survivors continued to cling to their battered land. By 132, sixty-two years after the destruction of the Temple, they had husbanded enough strength to rise again in a last, desperate revolt. The emperor Hadrian was forced to dispatch his best general, Severus, to quell it. And when the last Jewish bastion, Bethar, fell nearly three years later, it was said that the blood ran to the sea and that so many Jews were dumped on the slave markets that the prices plunged disastrously.

Mighty Rome had been troubled twice by this alien people. Hadrian would not have it so again. Their civilization would be expunged; the ruins of their city — and even its name — were to be obliterated. On its site, Hadrian built a small new city, a model of provincial Roman splendor. He renamed it Aelia Capitolina. Jews were banned from the place, and those who were caught defying the ban were to be summarily executed.

Atop the barren mound which had once been the Temple Mount rose an equestrian statue of the emperor facing a magnificent representation of his patron god, Jupiter Capitolinus. On the site of Golgotha, Hadrian is said to have had a temple to Venus erected to erase even the faintest stirrings of another alien tradition, the tiny Jewish sect called Christians whose seed had been planted there.

To underscore his conviction that the capture of Jerusalem was the outstanding achievement of his career, Titus ordered the construction of a triumphal arch in Rome. In the panel at left, a bas-relief from that arch, Titus's troops display the gold menorah taken from the sacked second Temple. Put to the torch by the Romans, the gutted building was soon consumed by flames — an event recorded in the Arab illumination below.

عشر صوم زوال النار عن البيت ومؤخر زج بحشيم عنه وترفع الجوس عن خزانه وهياكله

III

Jerusalem of the Cross

The man who most personified the triumph of mainstream Christianity over the "demon legions" of paganism in the fourth century was that "paragon of bodily strength, physical beauty, and mental distinction," Constantine the Great, ruler of the Eastern and Western Roman empires — a domain stretching from the shores of Britain to the banks of the Nile. When the emperor Diocletian — weary, in his words, of being "secluded from mankind" by his "exalted dignity" — abdicated on May 1, 305, to spend his remaining years raising cabbages in Dalmatia, a protracted civil war ensued among no fewer than six claimants to the imperial purple. Constantine emerged victorious in 323 after embracing the Christian god and marching into battle under the banner of Jesus. In gratitude, the pious monarch dedicated his empire to the credo of the new faith — and thus established Christianity as one of the world's enduring religions.

On a memorable day three years later, Constantine strode across the boundaries of the thousand-year-old city of Byzantium, which perched on the shores of the Bosporus, the narrow straits dividing Europe from Asia. Some centuries earlier the historian Polybius had labeled the site "the most secure and advantageous . . . of any city in our quarter of the world." These were obviously Constantine's sentiments as well, for he seized a spear and etched into the ground the limits of a new capital to supersede Rome and preside over the precincts of Christ on earth. The engineers and architects who walked respectfully behind the sovereign expressed amazement at the extent of the new outer boundaries he was tracing along the shores of the Bosporus. "I shall still advance until He, the invisible

guide who marches before me, thinks it right to stop," the emperor retorted.

Four years later, on May 11, 330, Constantine officiated at a solemn service of dedication for his New Rome — Constantinopolis. Like the old capital in the west, Constantinople boasted seven hills, was divided into fourteen administrative wards, and used Latin as the language of its government bureaus and courts. Like Rome, it was to be adorned with monumental buildings whose solidity and magnificence reflected the character of the splendid Byzantine Empire. An inscription incised at the emperor's command on the great column of porphyry in the Forum of Constantine proclaimed: "O Christ, Ruler and Master of the World, to Thee have I now consecrated this obedient city and this scepter and the power of Rome. Guard and deliver it from every harm."

Several years after the emperor had dedicated Constantinople to the cause of Jesus, a lone pilgrim passed through the city en route to Jerusalem. We do not know his name, but his anonymous chronicle has survived. It is the earliest known account of Christian pilgrimage to Jerusalem, where, three centuries before, the Apostles had planted the seeds of the primitive church in the ground on which Jesus had been crucified.

The Bordeaux Pilgrim, as he is known, was one of the earliest of the countless voyagers who were to brave the hazards of highway and sea because they believed that "they had less religion, less knowledge, and had not . . . the finishing stroke of their virtues, unless they had adored Christ in those places whence the Gospel had first shone forth from the Cross." In his travels, the

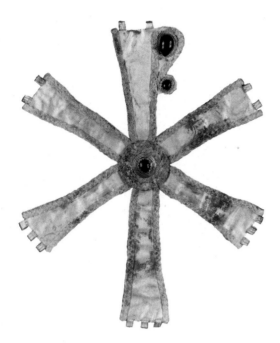

In the hands of Byzantine goldsmiths, Jesus' monogram in Greek — Chi Rho — became an elegant and decorative emblem set with garnets.

anonymous pilgrim covered 3,250 miles. His itinerary notes 190 stops and 360 changes of horse. Setting out from Bordeaux, he followed the Garonne River to Toulouse, turned north through the valley of the Rhone to Valence, moved eastward across the Cottian Alps into Italy, and passed through modern Yugoslavia, Bulgaria, and European Turkey to the city of Constantine. He then crossed the Bosporus into Asia Minor, where he rode south, following the Syrian and Lebanese coastline to the Holy Land.

The Bordeaux Pilgrim found a Jerusalem that was, in many respects, the same compact provincial settlement erected by Hadrian two centuries earlier over the ruins of the first and second Jewish revolts and renamed Aelia Capitolina. It followed the typical Roman town plan, which divided a city into four parts or quarters by a *Cardo Maximus,* or main north-south street intersected by an east-west thoroughfare. The lines of today's El-Wad, the lane running south from the Damascus Gate, and David Street, which runs east from the Jaffa Gate, roughly follow the course of those ancient streets.

Probably no more than five thousand people lived within Aelia's stout walls, which approximated the circuit of today's Old City ramparts. With the dispersion of the Jews, the Holy City had faded into near obscurity; the center of Roman life in *Provincia Palaestina,* as it had been in the days of the procurator Pontius Pilate, was Caesarea on the coast. But the Bordeaux Pilgrim's arrival coincided with an historic awakening for the Holy City. The pious Constantine had resurrected the old name Jerusalem, and he had also issued a fateful series of commands that would not only restore its ancient grandeur but seal the claim of Christendom upon the City of the Savior.

Thus the pilgrim was an eyewitness to Jerusalem's rebirth, both as a spiritual center and as an objective of religious pilgrimage. His account reveals a Jerusalem in which, for the most part, a rich body of Christian tradition was still waiting to be shaped. There was as yet no Via Dolorosa with its fourteen stations, no relics to touch or kiss, no birthplace of the Virgin Mary or *Coenaculum* of the Last Supper. Indeed, awareness of that latent Christian tradition was so unformed that the pilgrim omitted both Nazareth and the Sea of Galilee from his itinerary.

In his circuit of the Holy City, the pilgrim does mention the Pool of Bethesda along the eastern wall. It was there, the Gospel of John tells us, that Jesus raised a seemingly incurable invalid from his pallet and healed him. The great dais of stone and fill nearby that had once supported the Jewish Temple was still revered by the small Christian community, and the pilgrim devotes a good deal of comment to it. He writes that he saw there the pinnacle of the high southeast corner, where Satan tried to tempt Jesus. He also describes "a crypt in which Solomon used to torture devils," and "the blood of Zacharias which was shed upon the stone pavement. . . . There are also to be seen the marks of the nails in the shoes of the soldiers who slew him . . . so plain that you would think they were impressed upon wax." In this respect the early traveler from Bordeaux was no less credulous than many who would follow him.

What of the Jews? Evidently Constantine's policy of toleration also included a slight easing of the enforcement of the cruel sentence imposed by Hadrian — banishment from Jerusalem for all time upon pain of death. They could now visit the site of their ruined Temple and mourn its loss once each year — on the anniversary of its destruction, the ninth day of the Hebrew month Ab. The Bordeaux Pilgrim tells us that there was "a perforated stone, to which the Jews come every year and anoint it, bewail themselves with groans, rend their garments, and so depart." It was at the sacred rock that the Jews poured forth their grief in the fourth century. Later, when the Christians took to looking upon the Temple platform as polluted ground and converted it into a midden, the Jews sanctified the more remote Wailing Wall.

The pilgrim also tells of seeing "the house of Caiaphas the priest . . . a column against which Christ was beaten with rods . . . the *praetorium* of Pontius Pilate . . . a stone at the place where Judas Iscariot betrayed Christ. . . ." But his special awe is reserved for two basilicas "of wondrous beauty" built "by the command of the Emperor Constantine." One stood atop the Mount of Olives; the other was on the site of the Passion itself: "On the left hand is the little hill of Golgotha where the Lord was crucified. About a stone's throw from thence is a vault wherein His body was laid, and rose again on the third day." The emperor also memorialized the place of the Nativity, for the pilgrim records that in Bethlehem a third basilica was erected by royal command.

The foundations of Constantine's monumental project to consecrate Jerusalem to Christ were laid in the summer of 325 at a church council at Nicaea in Asia Minor, on the shores of beautiful Lake Ascania. To this

place Constantine had summoned the bishops of the Christian world — "a vast garland of priests," as Eusebius, the early Church father, describes them, "composed of a variety of the choicest flowers" — to reconcile a number of pressing doctrinal questions that were threatening to sunder the fabric of the Holy Church.

One of the principals at the council, Bishop Macarius of Jerusalem, sought out the Empress Helena, Constantine's mother, whose influence at court had waxed with her advancing age. Born a pagan and the daughter of an innkeeper, she had been converted by her son, who so revered her that he renamed her birthplace Helenopolis and had gold coins struck bearing her likeness and the inscription "Flavia Helena Augusta." Macarius told the empress of the abysmal neglect that had shrouded the sites of Jesus' birth, Passion, and Resurrection for some 300 years. To locate and enshrine these sites, to accord Jerusalem the singular honor due it as the fountainhead of Christianity, was surely the greatest contribution the imperial family could make toward the preservation of the young faith, the bishop argued.

Persuaded by his rhetoric, the eighty-year-old empress set out for the Holy City immediately with Macarius as her guide. Helena sallied forth armed with the imprimatur of the enthusiastic Constantine and supplied with funds sufficient to start the necessary work. Together she and Macarius identified a rocky grotto in Bethlehem as the site of the Nativity, climbed the Mount of Olives to stand where Jesus had instructed his disciples, and decided that Hadrian's temple to Venus concealed the true location of Golgotha, or Calvary, where Jesus had been martyred. Upon her return to Constantinople, Helena detailed her findings to the emperor. From them stemmed the Church of the Nativity in Bethlehem, the Church of Eleona — which means "on Olivet," as the Mount of Olives was then called — and the Church of the Holy Sepulcher. The empress's astounding discoveries confirmed Jerusalem as the holiest city of the Christian world, and they gave the aspiring pilgrim an earthly quest.

It was clearly Constantine's intent to make the city an enduring object of pilgrimage, and he was quick to memorialize his mother's findings. The place of the Crucifixion most fired his imagination: Eusebius tells us that the emperor hastily ordered that all traces of the pagan temple on Golgotha be expunged and "that the material of that which was destroyed, both stone and wood, should be removed and thrown as far from the spot as possible. . . ." When this work was done, a cave appeared — surely, it was decided, the tomb owned by Joseph of Arimathea, the tomb from which Jesus rose from the dead. When news of this reached Constantine, he wrote to Macarius that no power of language seemed worthy to describe this wonder. "Make provision for everything necessary," the bishop was told, "that not only shall this basilica be the finest in the world, but that the details also shall be such that all the fairest structures in every city may be surpassed by it."

Eusebius, an eyewitness to the construction, lovingly described the Byzantine masterpiece that resulted. The basilica, called the Martyrion, "reared to an immense height. . . . The walls outside exhibited a spectacle of surpassing beauty. . . . The inside was finished with carvings of panel work like a great sea . . . richly carved

49

Military conquest, royal caprice, and natural calamity have all wrought their effects upon Christendom's most hallowed structure, the Church of the Holy Sepulcher in Old Jerusalem. Sundered by repeated earthquakes, battered and ransacked by besieging armies, and defiled by non-Christian conquerors, the church has nonetheless endured. Beneath its clustered domes lie the traditional sites of Calvary and of Jesus' tomb. The structure that encloses both also serves as the terminus of the pilgrim trail that links the Stations of the Cross, one of which is seen at left above. The church and its sundry side chapels are administered by Latin, Syrian, Armenian, and Greek Orthodox seminarians, with the Greeks playing the most significant role. They oversee the altar (left) that now stands on the leveled site of Golgotha, the mound upon which Jesus was crucified, and they also conduct services in the Katholikon, or cathedral proper (opposite). At the end of the rotunda adjoining the nave stands the ædicula (above), the carved marble entrance to the sepulcher itself. Illuminated scrolls stand sentry before the portal, a tasteless 1810 addition to the church's already cluttered and eclectic decor.

An elevated slab of red limestone (below) marks the spot where Jesus' corpse was hastily embalmed after the Crucifixion. The Stone of the Anointing, as it is called, stands near the present entrance to the much-transfigured Church of the Holy Sepulcher. Traces of the original entrance to Constantine's basilica still exist, having survived the demolition ordered by the Fatimid caliph Hakim the Mad in 1009. Today these soot-begrimed pillars (lower right) are found in the storeroom of an Arab sweetshop near the church (right).

and gilded; and being overlaid throughout with radiant gold, it made the whole temple as it were to glitter with rays of light. . . ."

The basilica as a construction form had emerged from the architectural tradition of paganism. Adopted by the early Christians for their churches, it was a large hall divided into aisles by rows of columns. The central aisle, or nave, culminated in the altar, at which the deacons presided. A semicircular apse roofed by a half dome held the bishop's throne, or *cathedra,* which was flanked by the presbyters' benches.

Running east to west, Constantine's great basilica fronted on the pillared *Cardo Maximus,* where a marketplace stood in Eusebius's time. Remnants of the original entrance are still visible today — in, of all places, the vaulted storeroom of an Arab sweet shop. That entrance once led to an atrium, or colonnaded forecourt. Behind it lay the Martyrion, whose dome, Eusebius tells us, was supported by twelve columns — "equal in number to the Apostles of the Savior." The pillars were surmounted by silver capitals donated by Constantine. Immediately west of the Martyrion lay a second colonnaded court containing the rock of Golgotha. The church complex culminated in the Anastasis, the place of the Resurrection. At first it apparently was a round enclosure — open, in Eusebius's phrase, "to the pure air of Heaven." Later it took its present form, a rotunda enclosed by a huge dome. The structure was lavishly adorned with gold, silver, precious gems — and, undoubtedly, the mosaic decoration of unsurpassed workmanship at which the Byzantines excelled. Apparently the great church had not yet been formally dedicated at the time of the Bordeaux Pilgrim's visit in

333, for these formal offices seem to have constituted the climatic event of Constantine's Tricenarium three years later — the thirtieth anniversary of his assumption of power as Emperor of the West.

The most famous of the numerous legends surrounding Helena's pilgrimage to Jerusalem was her miraculous discovery of the True Cross lying in a rocky recess very close to Golgotha and the tomb. Whatever the facts behind the Invention of the Cross, it had become the central relic of the Good Friday ritual at the great church by the time an ascetic from Aquitaine named Saint Silviae reached Jerusalem in 385, some 60 years after the empress's visit. Silviae relates:

> The bishop, as he sits, takes hold of the extremities of the holy wood with his hand, and the deacons, standing around, guard it. . . . The custom is that every one of the people . . . kiss the holy wood, and pass on. . . . One time a person fixed his teeth in it, and so stole a piece of the holy wood, [and] it is now guarded by the deacons standing round, so that no one who comes may dare to do such a thing again.

At roughly the same time, Archbishop Cyril of Jerusalem, who had been ordained a deacon by Macarius, established a Holy Week rite for the pilgrims who had begun to flock to the city in ever-growing numbers. It included a procession from the Mount of Olives to the Anastasis on Palm Sunday; this evolved into the later ceremony of the Way of the Cross.

By the end of the fourth century, paganism was on the wane in Rome itself, where the leading families fell under the sway of a church father named Jerome who exhorted them to abandon their godless existence

The spectacular climax of Empress Helena's fabled pilgrimage to the Holy Land — a royal progress marked by the identification of the purported sites of the Nativity, the Sermon on the Mount, and the Crucifixion — was the discovery of the True Cross. In the colorful fresco at right, the octogenarian empress appears as a youthful and curiously androgynous onlooker, surrounded by her party.

and lay aside the burdens of earthly wealth. Their salvation, he preached, lay in embracing the Cross and in the selflessness of true asceticism. Under the watchful eye of a Christian emperor, the senate, in an unprecedented act of wholesale conversion, condemned pagan worship in a formal vote and adopted Christianity by a huge majority. Rome's leading patricians, the Anici, the Paullini, and the Gracchi, "were impatient to strip themselves of their pontifical garment; to cast off the skin of the old serpent, to assume the snowy robes of baptismal innocence," wrote one contemporary. Asceticism became the fashion as aristocratic converts renounced the pleasures of society, devoted their wealth to good works, and set off on pilgrimages to distant Jerusalem.

One such exemplar was a thirty-four-year-old Roman noblewoman of ancient lineage and high rank named Paula, whose journey to Jerusalem in 382 was immortalized in a chronicle written by Saint Jerome himself. In his description of Paula's visit to the Church of the Holy Sepulcher, we hear again of the True Cross and also learn of a new relic of faith, the stone that was rolled away from the mouth of Jesus' tomb.

The fate of the empire and Christianity now lay in the East, for tottering Rome was sacked by the barbarian Goths in 410. As imperial authority collapsed in the West, many Roman aristocrats took refuge in Jerusalem, enriching the city with their presence, their private residences—which Saint Jerome could hardly call austere — and their munificence. They were joined by patricians from the capital of the Eastern Empire, Constantinople. The most notable of these noble

Under Justinian I and his headstrong and politically astute empress, Theodora (below), the revival of interest in the Holy Land reached its apogee. The emperor, whose equestrian portrait dominates the medallion at right, initiated construction of dozens of hospices, churches, and monasteries along the pilgrim route laid down by the empress Helena.

émigrés was a refugee from the misfortunes of Byzantine politics, the "fair and exalted" Eudocia, wife of the Emperor Theodosius II and daughter of the renowned pagan Athenian philosopher Leontius. The empress, a brilliant and ambitious woman, had aroused the mistrust and hostility of her husband by becoming embroiled in a murky power struggle at court. Having embraced Christianity before her marriage, she chose to flee to Jerusalem. Hard on her heels was the emperor's confidential agent Saturninus, who had been dispatched to spy on her.

On Saturninus's orders two of Eudocia's friends, a priest named Severus and a deacon named John, were murdered. Eudocia retaliated by luring Saturninus to her home and stabbing him to death with her own hands. Deprived of the crown and condemned to permanent exile, she turned her imperial talents to the Christianizing of Jerusalem, becoming the veritable sovereign of the city. She built and dedicated a great basilica to the memory of the martyred Saint Stephen, founded a church on the site of the house of Caiaphas, and enlarged the city walls to encompass the Gihon Spring (which the Christians called the Fountain of the Virgin), the Pool of Siloam, Mount Zion on the west, and Ophel, the original City of David, on the east. She founded or restored a number of other churches, and she was influential in permitting Jews to return and settle. They became traders, craftsmen, and, as Old Testament scholars, guides to Christian pilgrims.

Under one of the greatest of all the Byzantine monarchs, Justinian I, and his flamboyant empress, Theodora, the revival of the Holy Land and Jerusalem

reached its zenith. The country prospered, enjoying a vitality it had not experienced since the days of Herod the Great. There were perhaps three to five times as many settlements as in any earlier period. Pilgrims became an unlimited source of new revenue, and even the desert region of the Negev in southern Palestine flourished, supporting six large cities, a thriving system of farming and irrigation, and a level of population unknown to the region either before or since.

Justinian built and endowed monasteries, churches, and hospices for pilgrims throughout the land, including one at Mount Sinai. The sixth-century Byzantine historian Procopius tells us that the emperor raised a church in honor of the Virgin Mary in Jerusalem "to which no other can be compared." So large were the blocks of stone hewn for it that each had to be carried from the quarry on a wagon drawn by forty specially picked oxen.

The star of Jerusalem blazed over the Christian world. Pilgrims, monks, nuns, hermits, and clerics flocked to its houses of worship, monasteries, convents, infirmaries, and holy shrines. By the late sixth century pilgrims were recording the existence of a body of ancient relics in the repository of Constantine's Martyrion that included the True Cross, the Crown of Thorns, the Reed, the Sponge, the Holy Lance, the Stone of the Sepulcher, and the Cup used at the Last Supper. If aids to faith were needed, the Holy City was more than able—and also more than willing—to supply them.

Despite Constantine's imprecation to his new-found deity to guard the Eastern Empire "from every harm,"

the Byzantine Empire would no more be spared from tribulation than was the Western Empire. After Justinian, the empire weakened under a series of "passing phantoms" who were confronted by proliferating military and political problems on their borders, domestic cleavages, despotic takeovers, and disruptive religious schisms over the nagging doctrinal question of the nature of Christ. Even more threatening was the rise of the new Sassanid Empire of Persia, whose Zoroastrian kings were as zealous in their desire to evangelize their faith as were the defenders of Christendom in Constantinople.

The Byzantine administration reacted to the Sassanid threat by centralizing its grip on the empire's outlying provinces. Onerous taxes were imposed, further fueling the discontent of the citizens of Syria, Palestine, and Egypt, the richest provinces of the empire. As might be expected, fearful emperors sought a scapegoat for their woes. And as before, that scapegoat was found in the Jews, against whom a reign of terror was unleashed.

Khosrau II of Persia (as we have seen in Chapter I) chose this moment to expand westward. He unleashed a devastating offensive toward the Byzantine Empire that nearly drove Heraclius from Constantinople. Only the persuasive power of Patriarch Sergius, coupled with a massive war loan from the Church, dissuaded the emperor from moving his entire court to Carthage.

Many of Heraclius's disgruntled subjects openly welcomed the Persians. These included Christians of dissident sects, who bore little love for members of the Orthodox Church. Oppressed Jews enlisted in the Persian ranks—and it was Jews within the walls who opened the gates of Jerusalem to the invaders in 614 after a siege of only twenty days. They then joined in ravaging the city.

Not since Titus and his legionaries had overturned the Temple and decimated the Jewish population more than five hundred years earlier had Jerusalem known such carnage. The Persians systematically demolished every Christian church and sacred shrine, including the Church of the Holy Sepulcher, Justinian's Church of Saint Mary Nova, and the buildings erected by Eudocia. The Church of the Nativity in Bethlehem escaped — but only, it is said, because the three wise men depicted in a mosaic above the entrance were dressed in Persian costume. The sacred relics, including the True Cross, were carted off to Ctesiphon. In an instant, the work of nearly three centuries had been undone.

Heraclius's crusade against the Persians was ultimately successful, and he was able to return to a liberated though ravished Holy City fifteen years later, triumphantly holding aloft the beams of the True Cross. But the victory was only temporary. The long war had sapped the strength of both victor and vanquished; their resources were drained and their long, inadequately garrisoned borders lay exposed and vulnerable to attack from any quarter.

The final blow came from the south. The tribes of Arabia rose as one under the war flag of Mohammed and Islam. Like the fiery winds of a desert *khamsin,* they burst forth without warning from the fringes of the bare yellow land. And the imperial armies of the Christian Byzantine Empire and the legions of Persia melted before them.

Jerusalem's once-bright future appeared seriously imperiled in 614 when a Persian army led by King Khosrau II seized the city. Soon thereafter Emperor Heraclius launched a fifteen-year campaign to rout the Persians and restore the city's ravaged shrines. The dogged emperor's ultimate triumph — and the subsequent assassination of Khosrau — are the subject of the champlevé enamel panel seen below.

IV
The Mosque of Omar

For aeons, tides of great change swept across the face of the Near East. Occasionally, where they touched the coastal fringes of the vast Arabian peninsula, civilization flourished. But for the most part the sun-blasted peaks and highlands, the steppes and barren deserts spanning most of Arabia's million square miles, lay beyond the pale of progress and change.

The Bedouin tribesmen who roamed the peninsula's trackless interior were suspended in a timeless existence, knowing little and caring less of empires, the rule of law, and the claims of nation-states. The Bedouin was the aristocrat of the wilderness. If nature had withheld the blessings of generous rainfall and fruitful soil, her abundant gift of freedom and self-sufficiency compensated for that lack. Even the claims of family, clan, and tribe were secondary to the nomad's sense of personal liberty, his appetites and passions, and the welfare of his horse, camel, and flock. His sheikh ruled only by sufferance; the chieftain without respect was cast aside. The Bedouin had no priests to minister to his fears or temper his lusts. Indeed, his camel was far more sacred than any man, for the beast could carry him five hundred miles in eight to ten days on a minimum of water. The Arab survived on the camel's milk and flesh; its dried dung served as fuel; its hair clothed him and supplied the material for tents. The date was the desert warrior's only other staple food. "Honor your aunt, the palm," later Moslems would say, "which was made of the same clay as Adam."

Blood ties to the social unit—the tribe—assured the Bedouin of only one thing: collective strength in the unending struggle for pasturage, water, and material sustenance. In his elemental code of existence, the property of other tribes was fair game. To possess it, raiding, looting, and even murder were sanctioned. Bedouin justice was equally elemental: blood for blood — or, occasionally, the payment of blood money in the form of a hundred female camels. In a serious feud, the quest for vengeance might widen to include the entire tribe to which the miscreant belonged. The tribal vendetta was the test of manhood, the inspiration for the noble odes of the Arab poet and balladeer. But it denied Arabia the sense of nationhood that had already bound most Eastern peoples.

The Arab precisely fitted the description of his legendary biblical ancestor, Ishmael, whom Islam would elevate to the status of patriarch. Like Ishmael — "a wild ass of a man, his hand against every man and every man's hand against him" — the Arab was sustained by plunder and ennobled by internecine war. Gambling, drinking, and wenching were the spice of his lusty life.

Far earlier than elders could recollect, the chieftains of Arabia had seen fit to ritualize an annual surcease from bloodshed. How else could a man pray or trade in peace? While eight months of the year constituted an open season on blood feuds and raiding, the remaining four were divided into two periods of holy truce. During the seventh month of the lunar year, and again during the final two months of the old year and the first month of the new, men could safely buy or sell goods at the trade fairs, or send laden caravans to the bustling market towns of Persia, Palestine, and Egypt. Through the annual markets of the Hejaz along the central Red Sea coast flowed the

This stele, carved in southern Arabia at the beginning of the Christian era, features a Bedouin tribesman and his herd of camels.

coveted frankincense of the Hadhramaut, the leather and fabrics of the south, the grain and finely wrought daggers of the northern tribes, the saddles of Hira, the swords and musk of India, and the gold and precious gems of Africa.

Each tribe clung covetously to its local divinities — who inhabited springs, trees, rocks, and stones — but during the holy truce, the paths of religion followed those of trade. Tribe upon tribe laid down its arms, left nomadic pasturages, and converged on the oases of the Hejaz. From time immemorial this area had been held as ground sacred to all — particularly the precincts and environs of Mecca, the most flourishing city of Arabia. Here men could not only trade at the teeming market but could also perform the cultic pilgrimage to the Kaaba, a square house of rude construction that served as the common shrine of all Arabian gods. As such the Kaaba was the home of more than 360 idols. Presiding over the pantheon was the image of Hobal, tutelary god of Mecca. Men also paid homage to an unusual oval stone of black basalt and red feldspar that had been built into the corner of the sanctuary. The Black Stone, seven inches in diameter, had already been worn oval in pagan times by the kisses of the pilgrims, who also engaged in cultic mysteries connected with a mountain called Arafat south of Mecca. Beyond language and custom, these were the only institutions shared by the tribes of Arabia prior to the sweeping politico-religious revolution led by the Prophet Mohammed.

Abulqasim Mohammed ibn Abdullah ibn Abd al-Mutallib ibn Hashim, born in or around the year 570, had one unique advantage: he belonged to an eminent branch of the tribe of Koreish, the lords of Mecca. Moreover, the family of Hashim had earned the honor — and concomitant income — of serving as the guardians of the Kaaba. However, Mohammed's liabilities seemed to exceed his assets. His father died shortly before his birth; his mother, when he was about six; the orphan's grandfather and guardian, two years later. Mohammed was illiterate, and his only direct exposure to the great civilizing forces outside Arabia was the result of two brief caravan trips to Syria. The first he made as a youth of twelve; the second, thirteen years later, as business agent for a comely forty-year-old widow named Khadija, who was to become the first of Mohammed's eleven wives.

According to some possibly hostile sources, Mohammed as a youth was given to recurring fits, possibly the result of epilepsy or an affliction of the nerves. It was not until he was forty that Mohammed began his personal search for spiritual certainty, after a life of desperate loneliness and paralyzing self-doubt. According to legend, he found that certainty in a cave on Mount Hira, in the bleak and desolate hill country several miles outside Mecca. There, during meditation, the call came: "Magnify thy Lord! The abomination — flee it! And for the Lord — wait thou patiently."

When Mohammed undertook his ministry against idolatry, only patience and sheer will enabled him to survive the persecutions of his fellow Koreish, who succeeded in driving him and a tiny handful of followers from Mecca to Medina, some 210 miles to the north. Mohammed, they cried accusingly, "hath said opprobrious things of our gods, hath upbraided us as fools, and hath spoken of our forefathers as hopelessly

اشتدی دو یامدی غیرت ایتدی جماعتندن ایلرو
کندی عقبه نول فتنه کلدی برچ سوز انو حقندا

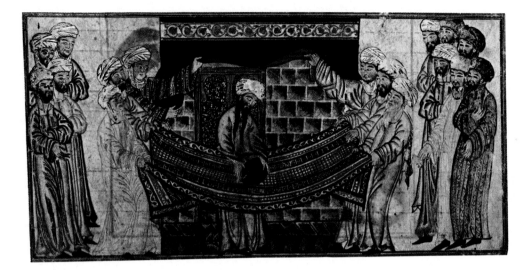

lost." To which the Prophet replied: "If they should place the sun on my right hand and the moon on my left to turn me aside, I will not desist, until that Allah make manifest my cause, or else I perish in the struggle."

The date of Mohammed's historic Hegira — the flight to Medina on which the Moslem calendar is based — was July 2, 622. Among the few converts who joined him were a prosperous merchant named Abu Bakr who had abandoned his wealth for the cause of Islam; Omar ibn al-Khattib, a giant of a man who had been a Koreish notable until his conversion; a friend named Othman ibn-Affan; and Ali, the Prophet's young cousin. These men were to become, in their turn, the four great caliphs of early Islam. Within four decades of the Hegira, they would plant Mohammed's standard throughout the Middle East, from North Africa and Egypt to the borders of India.

Only a handful of loyal supporters had fled with the Prophet to Medina, but an army of ten thousand followers marched behind him when he returned to conquer Mecca, convert the Koreish, and rededicate the Kaaba to Islam eight years later. As they marched they shouted: *"Ya Labbeik!"* — "Yes, Allah, we are here!" In those eight years, the bulk of the revelations of the Koran had been committed to memory by disciples, or copied by scribes onto parchment, palm leaves, or the shoulder blades of sheep. First Jerusalem, then Mecca had been designated the sacred *qibla*. The Night Journey to Jerusalem had become legend. The city's first primitive mosque — and the lusty voice of the ex-slave Bilal, the first *muezzin*, summoning the faithful of Medina to prayer there — had gained re-

nown throughout Arabia. Friday had been proclaimed the holy day of the Islamic week, and the month of Ramadhan had been dedicated to a stringent fast of atonement and to prayer.

The revolution of Islam demolished root and branch the near-anarchic social code, the polytheism, and the dissolute life-style of Arabia as thoroughly as Mohammed had expunged the 360 idols of the Kaaba. As for the Bedouins' life of license and indulgence, the Koran now intoned: "O believers! Verily wine, the casting of lots, and images and divine arrows are an abomination of the words of Satan. Shun them. . . ." Islam was as much a code of social behavior and obligation as it was a creed of faith. The easygoing Bedouin was suddenly bound to a single God, a single will, and, for the first time, a single purpose. It was no longer "legitimate," in the words of Mohammed, for a Bedouin "to appropriate anything that belongs to his brother." Under the temporal as well as spiritual leadership of the Prophet, the Arabs began to turn their aggressive energies outward — for as Mohammed preached in a sermon at Mecca shortly before his death in 632: "Know ye that every Moslem is a brother unto every other Moslem and that ye now are one brotherhood."

Islam's appeal to the men of the desert was simple, comprehensible, and uncluttered by dogmatic mumbo jumbo. To profess the faith one only had to say: *"La ilaha illa-l-Lah; Mohammadun rasuli-l-Lah"* — "There is no god but Allah, and Mohammed is his Prophet." The Koran was the holy revelation of Allah, delivered by the archangel Gabriel through Mohammed. The pure of faith were promised resurrection on the Judg-

ment Day and the exquisite pleasures of Paradise — an Eden graced with seventy-two magnificent, black-eyed *houris* (maidens), who lent a distinctly carnal note to the prospects of spiritual bliss in the afterlife.

To these few tenets were coupled five pillars of religious duty: to accept and regularly recite the profession of faith; to pray in the direction of Mecca five times daily (no mosque or priestly intercessor was necessary, only a prayer mat); to pay the *zakah*, or tax, in support of the poor and the mosques; to fast in the month of Ramadhan; and to become a *hadj*, or pilgrim, by undertaking the holy journey to Mecca — an obligation appropriated by Mohammed from the old pagan ritual.

To these five, some added a sixth obligation — *jihad*, or holy war. "War is ordained," said one oracle of the Koran from the critical Medina period, "even if it be irksome unto you." Another cautioned: "Prepare against them what force ye can, and troops of horse of your ability that ye may thereby strike terror into the enemy of Allah and your enemy."

The "enemy" had variously been the Jewish tribes near Medina, who were robbed, dispossessed, and in some cases massacred for refusing to follow Mohammed to the true faith — even though he had chosen to borrow freely from their Old Testament; the Koreish of Mecca, whose caravans had been plundered by the faithful; and, ultimately, some defiant tribes of the peninsula who held out tenaciously against the message of the evangelizing Prophet.

In 634, two years after the Prophet's death, the armies of Islam burst like a thunderclap from the desert into Iraq, Syria, Persia, Palestine, and Egypt —

the last of the great waves of Semitic conquerors. Like Joshua and the Israelites nearly two thousand years before them, the Arabs gazed in awe at the richness of the green lands, the comforts of civilized living, and the wealth and splendor of the mighty cities.

It was not only the glorification of holy war in the Koran or the enticing prospects of Paradise that drove this Islamic army forward, it was also the handsome prospect of rewards here on earth in the form of tribute from the coffers of the unbeliever. Arab appetites had first been whetted by the booty from the Koreish caravans and the conquered Jewish tribes of Arabia. The capture of the Jewish settlement of Khaibar, a hundred miles north of Medina, in the autumn of 628, had netted an immense plunder. All had shared the vessels of gold, jewels, stores of dates and honey, oil, barley, goats, sheep, and camels. As one Moslem poet wrote: "No, not for Paradise didst thou the nomad life foresake; Rather, I believe, it was thy yearning for bread and dates."

Following each Arab conquest the vanquished were offered four alternatives: conversion, tribute, imprisonment, or death. Tribute, the most appealing of the four, took the form of the *jizyah*, or poll tax. Only the aged and the young were exempt, and the immense wealth of the caliphs flowed in large part from such taxes. Only a little over a half century after the Hegira, Caliph Abd al-Malik, a descendant of the Bani Omeyya branch of the Koreish, was able to allot "the revenues of Egypt for the space of seven years" to the construction of the Dome of the Rock in Jerusalem, which was to replace the rude wooden mosque built atop the ruins of the Jewish Temple by Omar ibn

al-Khattib after the Arab capture of the city in 637.

It was not religious zeal alone that called the Holy City's most magnificent shrine into being, for Abd al-Malik, who ruled the Arab empire from Damascus, was a most practical man. It is true that in the earliest days of his ministry Mohammed had honored Islam's debt to Jerusalem by making it the first *qibla,* or direction of prayer. But later, after he was spurned by the Jewish tribes of Arabia, he made Mecca the focus of Moslem worship. To Abd al-Malik political urgency dictated that Jerusalem be restored to its former state of blessedness.

Mohammed had died in 632 without providing for a successor, and consequently the succession to the caliphate fell by election — first to Abu Bakr, then to Omar, Othman, and Ali. While the old comrades of the Prophet lived, continuity was assured, but then the unity of Islam was rent by a series of party and factional schisms — the ghosts of which haunt Arab politics to this day. One consequence was an insurrection in the holy cities of Mecca and Medina, the sacred seats of the movement itself. Under a despot named Abdullah Ibn al-Zubayr, rebels rose against the authority of the legitimate Omayyad caliphs. Abd al-Malik's predecessors had attempted to smash the revolt and regain control of the secessionist cities, but each had failed to do so. When Abd al-Malik ascended the caliphate in 685, he determined to bring his rival Ibn al-Zubayr to heel, for the despot was trying to undermine the very throne on which he sat. Pilgrims by the thousands had contrived to reach Mecca and Medina during the troubles, and their gold was filling Ibn al-Zubayr's treasury. Moreover, the renegade caliph was exploiting his considerable influence as ruler of the holy cities to win the political and religious allegiance of the pilgrims — and, through them, to mobilize the whole of Islam behind his cause.

Fearing for his own future, Abd al-Malik conceived a revolutionary scheme. He would divert pilgrims from Mecca and Medina, enticing them to the first *qibla,* Jerusalem. Rather than paying obeisance to the Black Stone of the Kaaba, they would pray at as-Sakhra, the sacred rock of the Temple, which they would circumambulate. It was to be a battle for the minds of the pious, and Abd al-Malik would use Ibn al-Zubayr's own weapon against him, even if it meant tampering with one of the five pillars of duty erected by the Prophet himself.

To lure the faithful to Jerusalem, the caliph would mobilize the most able Byzantine and Persian architects and artisans in his empire and command them to create a shrine to shelter as-Sakhra that would be unsurpassed for sheer magnificence not only in all the Islamic world but in the empire of the Christian infidels of Constantinople as well. The spiritual legacy of the Prophet might continue to inspire the pilgrims, but he, the caliph, would dazzle their physical senses. He informed his governors that he wished to "build a dome over the rock in the Holy City" from which Mohammed had ascended to the celestial spheres. He subsequently issued an edict forbidding his subjects to make the pilgrimage to Mecca. Jerusalem, he told them, "is now appointed for you" instead.

Next the caliph journeyed from Damascus to Jerusalem to inspect the site upon the great Temple platform — which the Moslems would call the Haram

Ash-Sharif, the Noble Sanctuary — and to convey his wishes directly to the two men who would oversee the project. They were Abul Mikdam Rija ibn Hayah ibn Jarul, famous for his great scholarship and wisdom, and Yazid ibn Sallam, a native of the Holy City. Abd al-Malik ordered them first to build a model of the plan which they had conceived for the Dome of the Rock; if it was truly worthy of his grand design, work might then proceed on the great sanctuary itself.

The relatively tiny prototype is called the Dome of the Chain, after King David's legendary chain of judgment, which could be grasped by the innocent but would evade the touch of the guilty. It was used first to house the treasure that financed the construction and later as a storehouse for the rare spices and incenses that perfumed the shrine. It still stands in the shadow of the great domed octagon, a monument to the monument it inspired.

It was absolutely vital to Abd al-Malik's scheme that the Dome of the Rock not only be built well, but quickly. Construction began in 687, and the structure was finished and dedicated only four years later. His overseers were economical as well as efficient, and as the work neared completion they reported to the caliph that 100,000 gold dinars remained unspent. Abd al-Malik generously replied: "Let this then be a gift unto you two for what ye have accomplished in building this noble and blessed house." "Nay," his faithful overseers demurred, "rather first let us add to this amount the ornaments of our women and the superfluity of our wealth, and then do thou, O Caliph, expend the whole in what seemeth best to thee."

It was eventually decided that the fortune Abd al-Malik's overseers had refused should be melted down and used to gild the entire dome. Such munificence had never been seen or imagined before, and the first Moslems to view the result must surely have thought that the caliph had captured the very fires of the firmament to adorn the great dome. Writing several centuries later, the Persian traveler Nasir i-Khusrau breathlessly described a blazing dome that "can be seen from the distance of a league away, rising like the summit of a mountain." Others would compare it to the sun or the moon. Two huge coverings made "of felts and of skins of animals" protected the burnished surface from the rains, snows, and winds of winter.

Two great domes then dominated the skyline of Jerusalem, attracting pilgrims from all over the world to the opposing poles of a mighty spiritual magnet: Christendom's Church of the Holy Sepulcher and the golden hemisphere of Islam's resplendent Dome of the Rock. Indeed, from the very beginning Abd al-Malik feared that Mecca and Medina were not his only rivals. The Islamic chronicler Muqaddasi tells us that the caliph noted the "greatness" of the dome of the Anastasis and "its magnificence," adding that he "was moved lest it should dazzle the minds of the Moslems, and hence erected above the Rock the Dome which is now seen there."

Abd al-Malik's fear that earthly vanities might sway the children of Mohammed to the cause of Jesus is the first evidence we have that the two great religions were already at odds with one another — although at this stage their competition was a bloodless one, waged in stone and mortar, and seemed harmless enough. That the caliph consciously tried to emulate the great

Church of the Holy Sepulcher in his design of the Dome of the Rock is clear from a comparison of the plans and measurements. In both a great rotunda culminates in a mighty dome that shelters sacred rock. In both the height of the supporting drum is equal to its diameter, which in turn is almost equal to the height of the dome. The inner diameter of the cupola of the Moslem sanctuary is roughly sixty-six feet, while the church's is sixty-eight feet. The heights of the domes are, respectively, about sixty-seven feet and about sixty-nine feet. Indeed, some two centuries later the Christian patriarch Thomas would be thrown into prison by the Moslems on the grounds that the dome of the Church of the Holy Sepulcher was slightly higher than that of the Kubbat as-Sakhra — a contravention of previous covenants granting freedom of worship to the Christians.

But if the Dome of the Rock was somewhat imitative of the monument to Jesus, it was also distinctive and evolutionary. Abd al-Malik was interested less in emulation than in uniqueness, and to provide it his architects turned to an ancient Roman innovation of which the Tower of the Winds at Athens and the Mausoleum of Diocletian at Spalato (modern Split in Yugoslavia) were contemporary examples — the octagon. The supporting drum and golden dome were to erupt, as it were, from an octagonal base. Four of the eight equilateral sides, pierced by porticoed entranceways, would be aligned with the cardinal points of the compass. The interacting faces of the octagon, drum, and globe would be united by a surface of brilliant mosaic — millions of colored cubes, like points of starglow. The caliph's Byzantine craftsmen

were consummate masters of the mosaic medium, and their bursts of yellow, red, blue, green, gray, black, and gold formed shimmering patterns against the cobalt blue sky.

But the dazzling exterior provided only a foretaste of the wonders that lay within, all of which were calculated to make the gaunt, pitted rock at the Dome's center appear to leap upward, as in Moslem legend, toward the heavenly Paradise. The interior was divided into three rings (see floor plan, page 70), the innermost of which was composed of the sacred rock, the drum, and the vaulting dome. Girdling as-Sakhra was a rich latticework screen of ebony wood, a curtain of fine brocade that could be drawn aside, and a circle of piers and columns supporting the rotunda.

Surrounding this circle were the middle and outer ambulatories, which were formed by an intermediate octagon of piers and columns whose lines paralleled the eight faces of the outside wall. The columns, all sculpted from the finest variegated and veined marbles, had been resurrected from the ruins of Christian churches leveled by the Persian king Khosrau more than seventy years before. The annular rings of supports were spanned by majestic arches whose spandrels and tie beams, like the arc of the inner dome high above, were richly adorned with mosaics, painted plaster, and jewels forming intricate designs as inventive and varied in form as the infinite imaginative powers of man himself. Hardly an inch was left undecorated.

The modern visitor is amazed, not only by the luxuriance of the decoration or the seeming vastness of the interior compared to the relatively modest size of

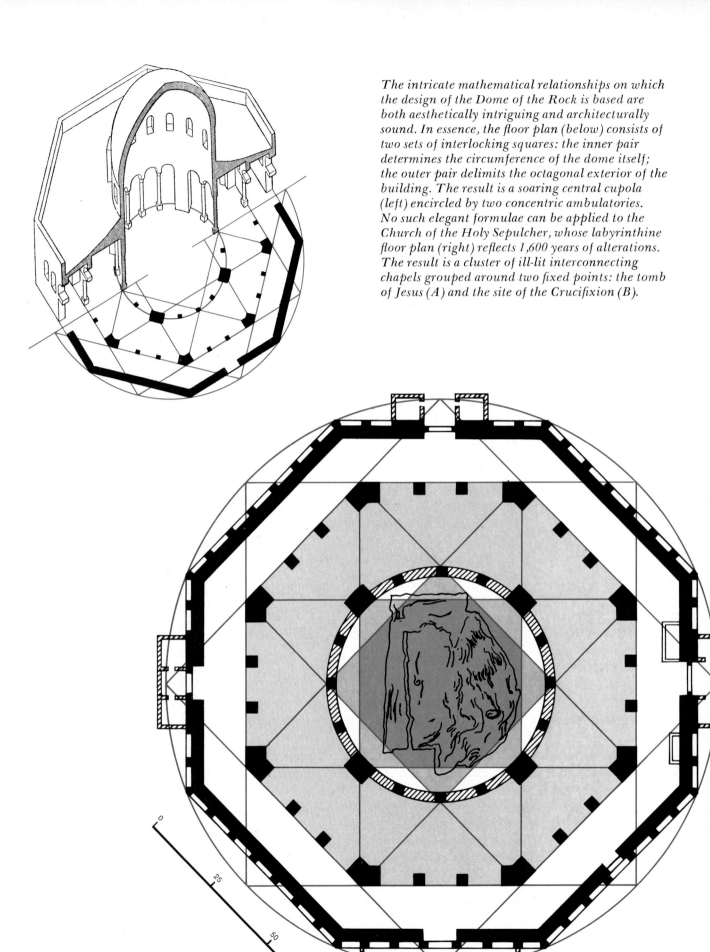

The intricate mathematical relationships on which
the design of the Dome of the Rock is based are
both aesthetically intriguing and architecturally
sound. In essence, the floor plan (below) consists of
two sets of interlocking squares: the inner pair
determines the circumference of the dome itself;
the outer pair delimits the octagonal exterior of the
building. The result is a soaring central cupola
(left) encircled by two concentric ambulatories.
No such elegant formulae can be applied to the
Church of the Holy Sepulcher, whose labyrinthine
floor plan (right) reflects 1,600 years of alterations.
The result is a cluster of ill-lit interconnecting
chapels grouped around two fixed points: the tomb
of Jesus (A) and the site of the Crucifixion (B).

0

25

50

65½ Feet

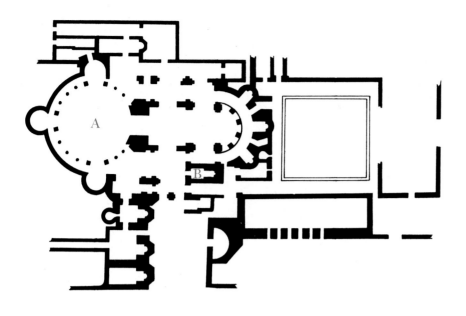

the exterior, but also by the incredible harmony of opposing architectural and decorative elements that should, by all reason, have evoked dissonance and tension. The horizontals, verticals, arcs, intersecting planes, and kaleidoscopic decorative surfaces meld into an awesome unity of design that seems to symbolize the essential harmony of disharmony — the oneness of life itself.

The perfect blending and balance of these incongruities work their way into the very soul of the beholder. The source of this subtle magic lies in elegance of proportion. This is both the genius and power of the Dome of the Rock, for each structural element and decorative pattern bears a fixed geometrical and mathematical relationship to every other element. Our subconscious minds take note of this satisfying relationship, even if we consciously do not.

The British authority on Moslem architecture Professor K. A. C. Creswell was one of the first to point out the amazingly simple concept on which Abd al-Malik's builders based every single measurement of their plan. Once the diameter of the circle of the central rotunda was established, two staggered squares were inscribed within it (see diagram opposite). When extended, the sides of these squares intersected and determined the dimensions of the octagonal lines of piers and columns that divide the ambulatories. When prolonged, the sides of the octagon itself formed two other staggered squares, which were circumscribed by another circle. An octagon inscribed in this circle and drawn parallel to the lines of the piers and columns determined the dimensions of the outside of the building.

Ancient architects and engineers had used such geometric formulas in the great pyramids of Egypt, in Greek temples, and in both Persian and Byzantine buildings. So marvelous were these formulas thought to be that they constituted a secret art, protected by dark and mysterious oaths. In the Dome of the Rock, the geometric conception reached the pinnacle of its development. Of its indefinable effect, Professor Creswell wrote:

Under a scheme whereby the size of every part is related to every other part in some definite proportion . . . a building instead of being a collection of odd notes becomes a harmonious chord in stones, a sort of living crystal; and after all it really is not strange that harmonies of this sort should appeal to us through our sight, just as chords in music appeal to us through our hearing. Some of the ratios involved . . . are fundamentals in time and space, they go right down to the very basis of our nature, and of the physical universe in which we live and move.

The ceremonials conceived by the caliph matched the magnificence of the shrine: each day and night fifty-two attendants worked to produce the precious compound called *khuluk*, one of the essences that perfumed the Dome. They pounded and pulverized saffron and then leavened it with musk, ambergris, and attar of roses from the Persian town of Jur, whose blooms were highly valued for their scent.

At dawn, attendants arrived to purify themselves in special baths. In the Dome of the Chain they changed into garments of rare cloth woven in distant Khurasan and Afghanistan, shawls from Yemen, and girdles of precious jewels. Bearing jars of the *khuluk* to the

In Abd al-Malik's day, the horns of a ram — ostensibly those of the animal sacrificed by Abraham 2,600 years earlier — hung suspended above the surface of the sacred rock. Today those relics have been replaced by floodlights, which cast a harsh light across the rock's pitted surface.

Kubbat as-Sakhra, they anointed the sacred rock with the aromatic mixture and lit censers of gold and silver that had been filled with richly scented aloes from Java, and incense compounded from musk and ambergris. Once the interior had been thoroughly bathed in fragrance, the attendants carried the smoking censers outside, where the wondrous odor of the incense could waft from the raised platform of the Haram to the bustling marketplace beyond.

Muezzins proclaimed: *"Allahu Akbar!* Verily, the Sakhra is open for the people, and he who would pray therein, let him come." Propelled to the Dome by all his senses, the worshiper savored the subtle aromas as his vision slowly adjusted to the muted lighting. The honey-pale rock was bathed in an unearthly sheen that filtered through the narrow windows of the high drum and flickered from hundreds of glowing lamps that burned the scented oils of the tamarisk and jasmine. He looked upward in awe at the great expanse of the dome. Suspended from its center hung a chain that held three singular relics — a lustrous, outsized pearl; the horns of the "Ram of Abraham," ostensibly sacrificed by the father of Ishmael on that very spot; and the crown of Khosrau.

Each worshiper slowly circumambulated the rock, savoring the heady delights of paradise on earth, performing two prayer prostrations before it, reciting the profession of faith in the one God Allah and his Prophet, and uttering appropriate verses of the Koran coupled with personal entreaties. He then returned to the pale of worldly Jerusalem, the rare scents of the Dome clinging to him like an invisible halo. As he passed through the streets of the city, passersby would

72

perceive the perfume and exclaim, "He hath been in the Sakhra."

Despite its grandeur, Abd al-Malik's conception would never displace Mohammed's. Mecca and Medina remained uppermost in the minds and hearts of aspiring pilgrims, for there the Prophet had been born, had prevailed, and had died. In time the Dome lost its original function, for Ibn al-Zubayr was defeated and slain. Yet through Abd al-Malik's wondrous building, Jerusalem became part of the essential itinerary of Moslem pilgrimage, and few chose to pass it by. Those who could not travel to Arabia came to the Holy City instead.

"Jerusalem, third in excellence," wrote the traveler ibn-Battuta, "God's honor be upon her." Abd al-Malik's builders had dredged through the storehouse of history for the notions and, in part, for the material of which the Dome of the Rock was made. But in the hands of Rija ibn Hayah and Yazid ibn Sallam, something new was born — and the building stands today as the foremost example of Islamic art. It is testament enough to the importance of Abd al-Malik's achievement that another great caliph, Abdullah al-Imam al-Mamoun, who reigned in the fabled city of Baghdad more than a century later, tried to usurp credit for building the Dome of the Rock by blatantly expunging Abd al-Malik's name and inserting his own in the dedicatory inscription that had been added to the building in 691, the year that the sanctuary of the Dome was finally finished.

The ravages of weather, time, and man eventually scarred all the stones of Jerusalem's churches and mosques. During periods of civil war and political upheaval in the Arab world, Moslems would find a scapegoat in the Christian holy places and engage in brief orgies of profanation and pillage. Earthquakes took their toll on the Haram, but damage was diligently repaired, deterioration checked, and the buildings restored. Change has always been a condition of Jerusalem's existence, and its numerous public buildings, manifestations of vibrant living faiths, have either adapted to it or perished.

This period, from the eighth through the tenth centuries, was a golden age for Jerusalem. Two unending streams of pilgrims, Christian and Moslem, marched to its gates, and the city thrived upon their wealth, energy, and piety. Christians no longer looked upon the arduous journey to the Holy City as merely a quest for "knowledge," but also as a task of penance for the remission of sin.

It was also an era of peaceful and productive collaboration between the Islamic Middle East and Christian Europe. The market of the Holy City developed into an Oriental hub of commerce in the goods and treasures of East and West. Each September, the merchants of Venice, Genoa, Pisa, Florence, Barcelona, and Marseilles flocked to the city's great trade fair, where they obtained the spices, incense, sugar and silks, exotic fruits and nuts, and dyed stuffs that Europe craved. Very early in the ninth century, the great Emperor of the West, Charlemagne, sought an alliance with Islam against the Byzantine Empire, and he sent a special embassy to the illustrious caliph Haroun al-Rashid, who inspired many of the tales of *The Arabian Nights*. After an exchange of wondrous gifts, al-Rashid placed all Christian pilgrims to the Holy Land under his personal protection and permitted Charlemagne to build a hostel for them in the Holy City.

Regrettably the entente was destined to collapse. In 996, an eleven-year-old Fatimid caliph named Abu Mansour al-Hakim ascended to the throne in Cairo. History assigns him to ignominy as Hakim "the Mad." During the early years of al-Hakim's reign, a eunuch named Barjewan wielded the real power in Egypt, contemptuously and indiscreetly referring to his sovereign as "the Lizard."

On April 15, 999, al-Hakim dispatched an ominous message to the eunuch: "The little lizard has become a huge dragon, and calls for thee." It was Barjewan's head that the monarch wanted — and received. The fateful eleventh century had begun.

Never before had Islam been ruled by such an eccentric and monstrous figure. Given over to excess and morbid sexual obsessions, al-Hakim forbade his subjects to appear on the streets after nightfall; banned the drinking of wine and the eating of honey, raisins, and dates; ordered all the dogs in Cairo slaughtered because a mongrel had snapped at his horse; and confined the women of the capital to their homes at all times, forbidding shoemakers from making shoes for them. Finally, he proclaimed himself divine, an incarnation of Allah himself.

In 1021, Hakim the Mad was assassinated on a hilltop outside Cairo — where he frequently retired in the evenings to worship the planet Saturn — on the orders of his sister, whom he had accused of unchastity. But the essential damage had been done. Before his death, al-Hakim had unleashed fearful persecutions against both Christians and Jews, forcing them to wear black robes and ride only on donkeys. He had issued edicts closing all the churches in his kingdom, and he had ordered the Church of the Holy Sepulcher razed to the ground, "that its earth shall become its heaven, and its length its breadth." An attempt was even made to hew to pieces the rock of the Tomb of the Resurrection. Christian Europe would long remember al-Hakim's deed — with the most profound consequences for the world.

In the year 1060, a great chandelier of five hundred lamps that hung from a chain in the Dome of the Rock fell and smashed upon the great rock, as-Sakhra. For Moslems in Jerusalem it seemed a sinister augury. "Of a surety," they said, "there will happen some portentous event in Islam."

V

Holy War in the Holy Land

In describing the selfsame historical event, the English historian Edward Gibbon spoke of "a new spirit . . . of religious chivalry . . . of exquisite feeling," while the Moslem poet Abi-wardi grieved over "a calamity that awakes the sound sleep." Both historian and poet were describing the Crusades — and both were right. The unparalleled saga of the thousands of Christian soldiers who marched eastward across the face of Europe behind the fluttering standards of the Cross to relieve the Holy Land of its "Saracen yoke" comprises one of the most stirring — and perhaps most shameful — chapters in the annals of man.

With each new call to arms, Western European theologians and clerics reassured their followers that they had resolved the moral issue raised by the biblical injunction "Thou shalt not kill." In Mohammed's time, that solution had been called *jihad* — the holy war to defend and propagate the faith. Several centuries after the Prophet's death, the popes of Rome also seized upon the concept of holy war. To die for the Church or for a cause sanctioned by the Church was to expunge the heavenly slate of one's sins. There was no want of causes to die for. At home, there were both Christian civilization's continuing struggle to resist barbarian onslaughts and the contest for territory between developing European nation-states. The Moslem tide had swept as far west as Spain, Sicily, and Italy — and it was threatening to spill across the Pyrenees from Spain into France.

Other trials of strength also occupied the European world at this time, trials to which the concept of holy war did not properly apply. In one such contest the popes of Rome, the see of Saint Peter, sought to regain from the Byzantine emperor and patriarchs the supremacy that their city had lost to Constantinople, "the New Rome." In the middle of the eleventh century, this power struggle between the Eastern and Western churches took the form of a series of ecclesiastical and theological disputes, and in 1054 the Roman Church went so far as to excommunicate the Patriarch of Constantinople.

In other areas, young noblemen vied for their king's favor or for family patrimony, while merchants from the Italian city-states — Genoa, Pisa, Venice — battled for control of the land and sea routes to the markets of the prosperous Orient. At the same time the peasants of France and Germany were struggling for sheer survival — against the hardships of drought, flood, famine, overpopulation, and the oppressions of invading barbarians and their own seigneurs.

In a number of ways, the East offered not only challenge and opportunity to the West, but salvation. One form of salvation in particular had been pursued by the devout of Christian Europe since the days of the Bordeaux Pilgrim and Empress Helena: pilgrimage to the holy places of Palestine. By the tenth and eleventh centuries, pilgrims in countless thousands were streaming eastward — by land through Hungary, Constantinople, and Asia Minor; by sea from Italy or France — to perform what had become a Christian duty.

Although tenth-century Jerusalem was under the authority of the Fatimid caliphs of Cairo, the city was by and large a spiritual condominium in which Moslem and Christian coexisted peacefully, for by then Moslem tolerance toward the other "Peoples of the Book" had been incorporated into the Islamic legal

The impact of the Crusades was felt as far away as Scandinavia, where this contemporary chessman was carved in the shape of a crusading knight.

code. Except for the stained rule of the fanatical al-Hakim, under which Moslems suffered as acutely as had Christians and Jews, the Fatimids had strictly observed the letter of the code. It was, in fact, al-Hakim's son al-Zahir who gave Byzantine Emperor Constantine VIII permission to rebuild the shattered Church of the Holy Sepulcher.

In this spirit of toleration, Christian and Moslem pilgrims shared Jerusalem. The latter gazed in awe at the Dome of the Rock, performed the prescribed rites around the gaunt stone of as-Sakhra, and prayed in the great mosque of al-Aksa, erected on the Haram's southern edge by Abd al-Malik's son and successor, Abd al-Walid. The streams of pilgrimage merged at such places as the Tomb of the Patriarchs in Hebron, one of a number of shrines held sacred by all three faiths. Writing about Jerusalem roughly a century before the First Crusade, the Arab chronicler Muqaddasi could say with pride: "All the year round, never are her streets empty of strangers. . . . The hearts of all men of intelligence yearn toward her."

Unhappily, the yearnings of intelligent and not-so-intelligent men tended in directions other than those of concord and coexistence as, for all the reasons cited earlier, the pent-up energies and discontents of the West sought a release outward. In the second half of the eleventh century, an explosive series of events shattered the stability of Western Asia and gave Christian Europe not only the provocation but the excuse it needed to thrust eastward.

Early in the century fierce bands of Turkoman nomads — called Seljuks after their eponymous ancestor — had burst out of Central Asia and swarmed into the territories of the two great Arab caliphates, the Abbasids of Baghdad and the Fatimids of Cairo. By 1055 the Seljuks controlled Persia, Iraq, and Armenia, and they had begun to overrun Byzantine Asia Minor, interdicting the land routes used by Christian pilgrims to reach the Holy Land. In the next fifteen years, the Seljuks were to establish themselves in Syria, and then turn their attentions to the empire of the Fatimids, against whom they waged an intra-Moslem holy war.

As relatively recent converts to Islam, the Seljuks were fervent proselytes — more Moslem than the Moslems — and they considered the brand of religion practiced by the Fatimids a heresy. In 1077 the Seljuks managed to wrest Jerusalem from the Fatimids, and they held it for more than twenty years. The Turks felt anything but sympathy toward the Fatimid code, which obliged Moslems to protect the freedom and interests of nonbelievers, and they acted promptly to suppress Christian worship in the Holy City. To the Christian West, it was as though Hakim the Mad had returned from the dead.

Two men, poles apart in origin, manner, and position, fully understood the impact of these events on Christian Europe. Both appreciated the potential enormity of the forces that might be unleashed if aroused, and both shared the charismatic power of impassioned oration, wielding words like a flaming sword. One had been born into a highly placed family in Châtillon-sur-Marne in France, had received the benefits of a distinguished ecclesiastical education, had swiftly risen to become Cardinal of Ostia, and, in 1088, had been elected pope. Tall, striking, distinguished, he used the eloquence of restraint and reason

Et auci
eunes hi-
toires di-
ent que
eracles·
qui mit
fu boin z
crestieus

ouuertot
lempure de
romme· ar
en son tep
oz a home·
auoit iael
te qui fu
messages

b dyables
d fist enten
dint qu'il
estoit pro
phetes· en
uoies de la
mecu el
tenps eu

The multipaneled manuscript illumination at left offered readers of Godfrey of Bouillon's history of the Crusades a visual recapitulation of key events in Jerusalem's early history. From top left, the panels include three views of Heraclius's conquest of the Holy City in 629; the rebuilding of the Temple; and the siege of Jerusalem by Omar. The last is a portrait of Peter the Hermit, the eccentric evangelist who preached the First Crusade to the peasants of Western Europe. That cause found a more eloquent and effective spokesman in Pope Urban II, who exhorted the delegates at the Council of Clermont (right) to liberate the Holy Land, crying "Dieu le veut!" — "God wills it!"

to move men as others might use the lash. He was Urban II.

The other is known to history only as Peter the Hermit. He was a simple Picard priest, probably from Amiens. Sources differ as to his antecedents — some maintaining that he belonged to a noble family and served as a soldier for a time; others, that he was of peasant stock. Later chroniclers tended to romanticize Peter's role, especially in relation to that of Urban, but even under these circumstances the profile that emerges is one of a highly volatile ascetic who was short, dark, homely, ragged, and emotionally unstable. Riding upon a donkey or mule whose fame among the peasantry was exceeded only by that of its rider, Peter traveled about Italy bare-headed, barefooted, and wearing the filthy cape that earned him the sobriquet "the Hermit." As he traveled, Peter evangelized, reminding the peasants of Western Europe of their Christian duty to Jerusalem.

About the year 1093, while the Turks were holding Jerusalem, Peter joined the ranks of the pilgrims. In one version of what followed, he is maltreated and robbed in Anatolia by the Seljuks, who force him to turn back. In another version Peter reaches the Holy City, where he is an indignant witness to the outrages committed against his fellow Christians, who are beaten, mocked, spat upon, overtaxed, and robbed. Seeing "the grievous misery of the poor devout Christians," Peter speaks to Symeon, the Patriarch of Jerusalem, who urges him to aid in mobilizing "the Christians of the West to the help of the Holy City." Symeon gives Peter letters to be delivered to the pope and to the sovereign heads of Europe, pleading for

"their aid for the recovery of those [holy] places out of the hands of those cruel infidels."

Whatever the exact circumstances, when Urban II rose before the assembled dignitaries at the Council of Clermont in the autumn of 1095, he was fully resolved that the West should and would deliver the aid that had been requested not only by clerics like Symeon but by the Byzantine emperor Alexius Comnenus as well. The infidel Turks were at the gates of Constantinople, the mother city, and the pope was aware that Christendom might not survive its fall. To Urban, the signs — as well as the opportunities — were clear: the Byzantine Empire had demonstrated that it was no longer worthy or deserving of its traditional role as defender of the cause of Christ and protector of pilgrims to the Holy Land. He was determined that Rome assume the task. As a result, Urban reasoned, the churches of the East and West would be reunited under the Latin pontiff.

The pope at last outlined his plan to the council; few orations have altered history quite so profoundly. So many flocked to hear the pope's announcement that they were directed to a field just outside the city, whence his throne was carried. Urban began by praising the bravery of the Franks, and then moved quickly to his theme. It was urgent that aid be dispatched to the Franks' suffering brethren in the East, in response to their urgent appeals. The Turks were advancing rapidly on all fronts, causing great distress not only to the Christians of the Orient but to those of the West who sought to make pilgrimages to the holy places of the Middle East. Churches and holy shrines had been desecrated — particularly those of

Jerusalem, which held a special place in the hearts of Christians and which must therefore be liberated for Jesus. This was God's work, and both rich and poor would share in it. All who took up the Cross would receive plenary indulgence or full remission of sins. There was hardship and evil at home; in the East there would be material rewards for the living and eternal rewards for those who died in the service of Jesus. Nothing must hinder them. God would lead them!

Throughout the fiery speech, members of the throng had punctuated Urban's oratory with the cry: *"Dieu le veut"* — "God wills it!" At the climax, the entire crowd, locked as one in the fervor of the exhortation to holy war, shouted: *"Dieu le veut! Dieu le veut!"* "Yes," the pontiff responded. "God wills it, indeed. He it is who has inspired these words. Let them be for you your only war cry!"

Adhemar, Bishop of Puy, rushed to the throne, begging to be the first to take the vow of the Crusade, and hundreds followed. August 15, 1096, the Feast of the Assumption, was designated as the time for the Crusaders' departure.

Before returning to Italy, the pontiff preached the Crusade in various parts of France. Princes, barons, and knights, led by the rich and aging Count Raymond of Toulouse, flocked to his call. The lists of the famous and infamous who pawned lands and treasures to raise knights and armies for the great Crusade included Godfrey of Bouillon, Duke of Lower Lorraine, a hero before his twentieth year under the standard of Emperor Henry IV; Baldwin, his brother, taller by a head than most men, who chose the eagle for his banner and coat of arms — and who was destined to become the first king of Jerusalem; Robert, duke of the illustrious house of Normandy and eldest son of William the Conqueror; Robert of Flanders, who pledged his duchy to his brother for five years for ten thousand marks; and the Norman adventurer Bohemund and his nephew Tancred, whose family had wrested parts of southern Italy from the Byzantines and Sicily from the Arabs — and who saw fair prospects in the Orient that had little to do with spiritual fulfillment.

The crusading delirium that caught up feudal barons and their knights in 1095 spread like wildfire among the deprived masses of France and Germany. It was Peter the Hermit, aided by his disciples, who recruited soldiers and pilgrims among the lower orders. Galvanized by Peter's frenzied evangelism — which turned desperation into hope and gave sudden purpose to aimless lives — farmers left their fields, clerks their stools, and artificers their benches.

All told, more than half a million souls, including perhaps 100,000 foot soldiers, participated in this unparalleled odyssey to the East. Old women, small children, and petty thieves joined an exodus compounded of both incredible selflessness and undiluted greed, seeking Christ and Mammon in a great rite of blood. It was blood that most found; less than 10 per cent set eyes upon Jerusalem. Some dropped off along the way to settle in the captured towns and cities of Asia Minor and Syria. Bohemund, for example, claimed Antioch, the city where the Disciples had first been called Christians a millennium earlier. Baldwin was for a time satisfied to remain behind as Count of Edessa.

Most of the Crusaders fell in battle, or were slain or

captured in ambush, or withered of thirst, starvation, disease, or stroke under the fierce Asian sun. Their bleached bones littered the stony soil, the mountain passes, and the sandy littoral — the road to glory and the Holy City — that ran from the shores of the Bosporus to the deserts of Syria. More than 17,000 hapless marchers — including women and children, the aged and infirm — were massacred in a Turkish ambush between Civetot and Nicaea. Another 4,000 were slain on the plain before Dorylaeum in a battle that cost the Saracens perhaps five times that many lives.

In barren Phrygia the Crusaders chewed on wild roots and sucked damp earth to assuage their hunger and thirst. Their horses and hounds deserted for want of water and forage, and they were forced to abandon their baggage. On one particularly frightful day, five hundred marchers dropped of exhaustion or sunstroke — or simply lay down and waited for death. And when the survivors finally reached the relief of a cool river, another three hundred perished from drinking too much too quickly.

Men were obliged to climb single file up the narrow, muddy mountain passes that hugged the steep defiles of the Anti-Taurus range on the threshold of Syria. The attrition of the march may have claimed more lives than the Moslems ever did. Soldiers and knights were encumbered by the weight of their chain mail coats, iron helmets, bucklers, shields, and swords, and they tried to sell them or simply threw them away. Men and animals slipped over precipices, and others merely sank and died of fatigue. Hundreds perished in a typhoid epidemic after the capture of Antioch.

The "Army of the Lord" also left a huge swath of devastation, pillage, and rapine in its wake, tarnishing forever the lofty purposes of its march to the East. At the very outset three German columns raised by Peter and his proselytes went on a bloody rampage through the valleys of the Rhine and Moselle. Led at times by a she-goat and at other times by a goose they thought was inspired by the Holy Ghost, the Germans tortured, burned, or put to the sword thousands of Jews — in Worms, Mainz, Trier, Neuss, and Prague. "Why should we, who march against the infidels, leave alive in Europe the enemies of our Lord?" their leaders reportedly cried.

Without order or discipline, the Crusaders pillaged settlements and farms of their own Christian brethren in Hungary and the Byzantine Empire. Despite the hospitality of Hungary's King Koloman, they sacked the town of Zemun and killed four thousand of its inhabitants. They raced through the streets of Belgrade in an orgy of looting, made off with stores of food, and set the city ablaze. After trying to do the same at Niš, they were attacked by the very Byzantine military unit that had been assigned to escort them safely to Constantinople, and five thousand Crusaders were slain. The leaders of the Crusade, those who had first harnessed their followers' discontents, suddenly found they were helpless to control the passions that had been unleashed. Emperor Alexius, who had asked for an army, found he had a wanton mob on his hands instead.

The hardiest of the crusading seigneurs found what they had come for — glory and power in the rich principalities of the Kingdom of Jerusalem. But soon quarrels, clashing ambitions, and endemic differences, both

*Plague, not Syrian bowmen, proved to be the real
enemy at Antioch, where thousands of Crusaders
were felled by disease (left, above) before they could
even reach the city's heavily fortified walls (left,
below). When the ancient stronghold finally
capitulated, a number of Crusaders encamped
there and refused to push on to Jerusalem. Thus
it was a sorely decimated and ragtag army that
surmounted the hill known as Nabi Samwil
(opposite) on June 6, 1099, and caught a first,
distant glimpse of its objective.*

among the barons and between the alien Latins and
the Byzantines, helped undermine the foundations of
the Crusader kingdom long before Christian swords
had finished carving out its boundaries. For instance,
no sooner had ancient Antioch, the gateway to Palestine, finally fallen to the Franks in June of 1098 —
after a harrowing series of misadventures — than
Bohemund demanded and received the coveted fief
for himself and his heirs. The Norman knight per-
severed over the bitter objections of Raymond of
Toulouse and in defiance of the Byzantine emperor
Alexius, to whom the Syrian city had previously been
pledged.

The climactic stage of the Christian quest led southward along the Syrian littoral, once the domain of
the trading and fighting fleets of the Phoenicians. The
Christian army bypassed the Moslem strongholds of
Beirut, Sidon, Tyre, and Acre; their turn would come
in good time, once Jerusalem, the object of the Crusaders' long ordeal, had been liberated for Jesus. The
hour was nearly at hand when, in the spirit of the Old
Testament verse, "the Lord shall have washed way the
filth . . . and cleansed the bloodstains of Jerusalem
from its midst by a spirit of judgment and by a spirit
of burning."

The thought quickened the steps of the 12,000 foot
soldiers, 1,300 knights, and perhaps 20,000 pilgrims
and camp followers — who were all that remained of
the vast numbers who had taken up the Cross in
distant Europe. They turned inland near Caesarea and
marched across the Plain of Sharon, where they began
the gradual ascent to the summit of the Judaean
Mountains. On Monday, June 6, 1099, the main col-

umn marched up the last rise of high ground separating it from Jerusalem. The next morning they stood atop the hill the Arabs call Nabi Samwil, the birthplace of the prophet Samuel, and saw silhouetted against the eastern sun the shadowy battlements, domes, and towers of the Holy City. As the Crusader-chronicler Raymond d'Aguilers relates:

> The Crusaders could not prevent themselves, in the fervor of their devotion, from shedding tears; they fell on their faces to the ground, glorifying and adoring God, who, in His goodness, had heard the prayers of His people, and had granted them, according to their desires, to arrive at this most sacred place, the object of all their hopes.

The profound tragedy of the ensuing five weeks was to haunt the Frankish kingdom until the end of its days — for it was not the Turks who waited behind the massive bastions of Jerusalem, but the Egyptian Arabs of the Fatimid Empire, who had retaken the city from the Seljuks during the preceding year. With the single exception of Hakim the Mad, the Fatimids had scrupulously observed both the letter and the spirit of the Islamic policy of toleration toward the Christians. During their benign stewardship of Palestine, Christians had worshiped freely in the Holy City; it was the recently ousted Turks who had abused that law, abridged those freedoms, and thereby sparked the First Crusade.

The Egyptians were as determined to keep Jerusalem as the Christians were to win it, for during the four centuries since Omar's conquest and the erection of the Dome of the Rock and al-Aksa, Jerusalem had become one of the centers of high Islamic civilization.

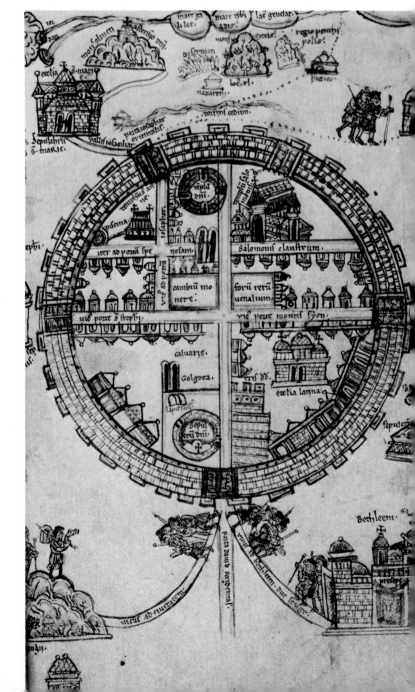

This Moslem culture, which illuminated the East and shed its light as far as Spain, would ultimately help ignite the Renaissance. The Haram area in particular was a great seat of learning; scholars, sheikhs, and the Sufi mystics who lent philosophic depth and profound humanity to the Islamic faith came from all parts of the Moslem world to study, debate, meditate, and pray at the religious retreats that huddled around it.

Under the Fatimid governor, Iftikhar ad-Dawla, preparations had begun early for the siege. Huge stores of provisions, heavy equipment, and arms had been collected, the walls had been strengthened, and outworks had been built on the vulnerable northern perimeter. The crack units of the Egyptian army that expectantly manned the city's defenses were, ostensibly, more than a match for the mounted knights and infantry of the Christians. Moreover, Iftikhar instigated a "scorched earth" policy throughout the surrounding countryside. The people of the villages and townships were herded into Jerusalem, doubling its population to 40,000. Crops were burned, herds and flocks dispersed, cisterns emptied, wells poisoned, and timber destroyed. The Crusaders found a wasteland. They also found, even at these heights, the shriveling heat of the *khamsin*, the superheated wind from the desert that seemed to drain water from the flesh faster than a man could replenish it.

The Franks were hardly prepared for an effective campaign, let alone a prolonged one. They had brought no siege engines from the plains below — no siege towers to surmount the city's walls, no battering rams to topple them, no mangonels to hurl missiles of stone against their defenders, and only a few ladders to scale them. It was as though the Latin barons had expected the forces of Heaven to reduce the city for them as they had interceded for Joshua at Jericho.

They pitched their camp on level ground north of the city and concentrated their strength along the northern and western walls. To mark their first Sunday at Jerusalem, the nobles made a pilgrimage to the Mount of Olives, where a Christian hermit prophesied the success of an assault on the following day. Accordingly it was launched, and failed pitifully — prophetic blessings being no substitute for adequate equipment. Shielded only by their bucklers, the soldiers rushed at the walls, trying to loosen the blocks with pikes, mattocks, and hammers. A shower of death rained on them from the parapets: arrows, spears, a hail of crushing stones, and, most devastating of all, "Greek fire" — a lethal mixture of flaming oil and pitch.

A few hardy souls managed to scale the walls on ladders, but their corpses were thrown back upon the heads of the besiegers. Night and heavy losses put an end to the feeble effort, and a council of war two days later reached the obvious conclusion — further assaults must await the building of siege machines. But where might the wood be found? Providentially, a Genoese fleet put in at Jaffa at this critical hour, bringing supplies, building materials, and skilled carpenters. Timber was discovered in a wooded area along the Nablus Road, and a second cache was found in a cave where it had been hidden by the Moslems.

The *khamsin* blew fiercely. Men licked the morning dew off the grass, dug into the ground to suck the moist earth, or drank the blood of their beasts. Some water was provided by the Gihon Spring, and more

was transported from the deep rift in which the Jordan flows, but neither supply could begin to satisfy the wants of the Christian army.

By early July, ladders, rams, mangonels, and three large siege towers were near completion. The fronts and sides of the towers were encased with iron and animal hides soaked in vinegar to ward off the Greek fire. On Friday, July 8, after fasting for three days, the bare-headed and bare-footed Crusaders began a solemn processional march around the city. Drawing upon the imagery if not the substance of the legend of Joshua, they raised holy chants to the heavens as they marched from the Mount of Olives in the east to Mount Zion on the west. All the while, the Saracens who crowded the walls hooted and jeered, aping the Christian chants and spitting upon crosses hastily made by the Fatimids for the event.

The main assault began on the night of Wednesday, July 13, in a shower of arrows. Iftikhar concentrated his return fire on the three great wheeled siege towers. "Greek fire" poured in flaming gouts from the parapets to keep the attackers from the walls. On Thursday, under heavy covering fire, the towers were slowly moved up, but by evening one was in ruins and the other two were damaged. "Miserable men that we are," cried Robert of Normandy, "God judges us unworthy of entering the Holy City and worshiping at the tomb of His son!"

The next day was Holy Friday — fittingly, or unfittingly, the Day of the Passion. The fighting began at dawn. Despite the spirited defense, one of the towers was pushed up against the wall near Herod's Gate, behind which lay the Jewish Quarter. Commanding the upper stage of the tower was Godfrey of Bouillon and his brother Eustace. Sometime between 9 A.M. and 3 P.M. — the sources vary — the tower's drawbridge was lowered and a Flemish knight named Lethold was able to establish a bridgehead atop the wall. Led by Godfrey, the Crusaders rushed in to support him. They cleared the breach of defenders so that others, scrambling forward with scaling ladders, could follow.

As soon as Godfrey's men succeeded in throwing open Herod's Gate, a group of soldiers led by Tancred raced down the narrow lanes toward the Haram Ash-Sharif, where Moslem soldiers were retreating to make a last stand — as had the Jews in Roman times. Tancred's speed confused and overwhelmed them before they could reassemble at the Haram, however. Pledging a heavy ransom, they surrendered, and Tancred's banner was soon flying atop the al-Aksa mosque.

The Christians wasted little time in stripping both al-Aksa and the Dome of the Rock of their wealth. According to the Arab chronicler Ibn al-Athir, Tancred's booty included forty large silver candelabra, seventy small lamps of silver and gold, and a huge silver lampstand. The tolerance of Omar, who had placed the Church of the Holy Sepulcher under his personal protection four centuries earlier, was not to be repaid in kind.

A detachment under Iftikhar, who had been successfully defending the southern wall against the assaults of Raymond of Toulouse, took refuge in the Citadel, which was then — and still is — referred to as the Tower of David. In exchange for a generous ransom, Raymond accepted their surrender and gave them safe escort out of Jerusalem. They were apparently

among the only Moslems to escape the fallen city.

It was the Jerusalemites who were held accountable for their enemy's three-year ordeal. The Crusaders ran amok, unleashing a wave of carnage and blind vengeance upon scarred Jerusalem. The slaughter continued through the evening, the night, and into the next day. Men, women, and children were slain where they cowered or as they milled frantically and aimlessly in the streets. Holy Jerusalem held no sanctuary for them; the tiny lanes, the houses, the suqs, and the mosques formed a vast abattoir. Even those who had been granted Tancred's protection at al-Aksa were hacked to pieces, as were the hordes of civilians who sought refuge in the Haram. The Jews moved instinctively in a body to their central synagogue, which was promptly turned into a funeral pyre.

The butchery went on until all but a few thousand were dead. Many of the victims lay in grotesque heaps in the vicinity of the Haram Ash-Sharif. One of the Christians who recoiled at the deed was Raymond d'Aguilers:

> Heaps of heads and hands and feet were to be seen throughout the streets and squares. . . . It was impossible to look upon the vast numbers of slain without horror; everywhere lay fragments of human bodies, and the very ground was covered with the blood of the slain. It was not alone the spectacle of the headless bodies and mutilated limbs strewn in all directions that roused horror in all who looked upon them. Still more dreadful it was to gaze upon the victors themselves, dripping with blood from head to foot, an ominous sight which brought terror to all who met them.

The Crusaders took possession of the houses of their choice by placing their shields upon the threshold or the wall. Then, sheathing their swords, they trooped to the Church of the Holy Sepulcher to offer up prayers of thanksgiving. It was Sunday, and Jerusalem was a Christian city once again.

There might have been a time, before the capture of Jerusalem, when Christian and Fatimid could have reached an accommodation based on common interest and the God that they shared. The Byzantine emperor Alexius had in fact counseled the Crusaders to strive for such a pact. But with the senseless massacre at Jerusalem, such hopes were abandoned. Around the bitter memory of that slaughter, the disunited Moslem peoples could in time coalesce. The flame of *jihad*, which had sputtered and died with Islam's consolidation, was rekindled. The new Christian state in the East had been born with its idealism drowned in blood, and with cancer already gnawing on its flesh and bones.

VI
Cross and Crescent

The first monarch of the Kingdom of Jerusalem, Baldwin I, coined a new motto to replace *"Dieu le veut,"* the war cry of Pope Urban II. It was "Christ conquers, Christ reigns, Christ commands!" The words rang with the heady confidence of men whose work would endure not for years or centuries, but forever.

The visible symbol of Christian permanence as masters of the Holy Land was the great golden cross that crowned the summit of the Dome of the Rock and dominated the skyline of Jerusalem. The city's newest masters had reconsecrated the Haram Ash-Sharif to the Savior, and knights, monks, and pilgrims thronged the great dais to gaze in wonder at the shining hemisphere of the Templum Domini, or Temple of the Lord, as the Dome was now called. Guides described the temple as the very sanctuary about whose precincts Jesus had conducted his ministry more than a thousand years earlier. The credulous pilgrims were also told that the al-Aksa mosque was actually the Palatium, or Templum Solomonis — "the palace which Solomon is said to have built."

The Cave of the Prophets, the grotto hollowed into the sacred rock in ancient times, had become a chapel variously called the Cave of the Souls and the Confesio; the depression in the rock that Moslem tradition identified as the footprint of Mohammed was now said to be that of Jesus; the Dome of the Chain was known at different times as the Church of the Holy of Holies and the chapel of the martyred Saint James. Wherever possible, all signs of Moslem origins had been expunged. The Christian conquerors, in linking each of the Haram's landmarks with their own tradition, had painstakingly blotted out every possible trace of its Islamic antecedents and associations.

What the Franks found expeditious to forget ate like a canker at the Moslem breast. In 1146, Nur ed-Din ibn Zangi, whom medieval Europe called Nureddin, ordered his master craftsmen to fashion a wondrous cedar pulpit, a masterpiece of high Islamic art, for installation in the mosque of al-Aksa on the day when all traces of the Christian infidel had been expunged from the Haram. The sultan Saladin, Nureddin's successor, took an oath "not to depart until he had honored his word and raised his standard" on Jerusalem's highest point.

At various times, Crusader rulers partially relaxed the ban on Moslem access to the Holy City. A cultured Syrian warrior named Usamah ibn Munqidh, lord of a great castle on the Orontes River known as Shaizar, could describe in his reminiscences a visit to the Haram and al-Aksa mosque around the year 1140, during a truce between the Franks and the Moslems. Usamah was permitted to pray in a small oratory that the Franks had converted into a chapel.

Although he numbered some among his friends, Usamah looked upon the Franks as "animals possessing the virtues of courage and fighting, but nothing else." Upon the intellectual and cultural superiority of the Moslems he based his hope of ultimate victory. Meanwhile, except for the occasional truces, there was little surcease for the kings of Jerusalem from the holy war that a new generation of determined Islamic rulers accepted as its foremost obligation.

At the zenith of its power, the Christian kingdom comprised the two isolated principalities of Edessa and Antioch in Syria, an inland corridor stretching south

The seal of the Knights Templar, a chivalric order founded twenty years after the conquest of 1099, features an Islamic dome capped by a cross.

through Palestine from Galilee to Hebron and the Negev desert, and every major port on the Mediterranean coastline from Gaza north to Tripoli and Latakia (see map, page 19). The Crusaders erected great castles on strategic heights to protect vital lines of communication between Christian cities and settlements or to interdict major Moslem overland routes. Their gaping hulks still dominate the landscape like forgotten megalithic tombs.

The Kingdom of Jerusalem, in historian Philip Hitti's phrase, was "a small Christian territory set against a vast and dark background of Islam." Travelers between the Christian enclaves were never entirely free from the dread of sudden Moslem raids or ambushes. The enemy lay within easy striking range of virtually every Crusader town, hamlet, and fort. The Latins remained a minority within their Oriental domain.

Throughout the war of attrition, the meager ranks of the Frankish nobility were further depleted by death and capture on the battlefield, and weakened by petty factionalism that the kingdom could ill afford. For a time the Saracens too were hobbled by intramural intrigues and civil wars in which petty rulers vied for the power to create a concerted movement strong enough to hurl the infidel into the sea. The result was a bizarre series of temporary political and military marriages of convenience in which Moslem and Crusader fought against Moslem and Crusader.

As Usamah's visit to Jerusalem suggests, the long struggle was leavened at times by amicable contacts and mutual accommodation. Trade and commerce coexisted with combat. Of this strange twilight zone, the Moslem chronicler Ibn Jubair wrote:

[Even] when the fires of discord burn between the two parties, travelers will come and go between them without interference. . . . The soldiers are at war, while the people are at peace and the world goes to him who conquers. Such is the usage in war of the people of these lands. . . . Security never leaves them in any circumstances, neither in peace nor in war.

Suspended precariously between conflict and thaw, Jerusalem nonetheless flourished. To encourage commerce within the city, Baldwin II decided in 1124 to remove taxes and duties for both buyers and sellers on goods imported to the Holy City, and to permit Moslems to market their wares. Venetians, Pisans, and Genoans, owners of the great merchant fleets of the West, were given unique trading monopolies in exchange for their naval support in the Crusaders' military operations. Despite the bloody events of 1099, Jews — in very limited numbers — were gradually allowed to return as artisans and traders. Reb Benjamin of Tudela, a Jewish traveler from the Spanish kingdom of Navarre, visited the city in 1163 and noted in his journal a community of some two hundred Jews who "dwell in one corner of the city, under the Tower of David." Most of them were dyers who purchased the exclusive concession in this craft from the king himself. According to Benjamin, these artisans were allowed to pray at the Wailing Wall. His is one of the earliest mentions of the tradition.

Merchants and travelers to Jerusalem sampled the exotic wares of its suqs and bazaars, shrouded from sun and rain by stone vaulting or canopies of canvas stretched across the narrow lanes. A flood of Western

Already weatherworn and deeply pitted at the time of the Crusader conquest, the sacred rock suffered further depredations under Baldwin I, first Latin king of Jerusalem and subject of the woodcut at right. Steps were chiseled into the rock (left foreground) and an altar was raised on its scarred surface. Souvenir vendors began hawking slivers of the stone to the pilgrims who flooded the Holy City, and Baldwin's successors were forced to cordon off the sacred rock to prevent its eventual demolition by relic hunters.

pilgrims enriched the coffers of Jerusalem's patriarchs and kings. Many settled, and John of Wurzburg writes of the city as a congeries of "Greeks, Bulgarians, Latins, Germans, Hungarians, Scots, Navarrese, Bretons, English, Franks, Ruthenians, Bohemians, Georgians, Armenians, Jacobites, Syrians, Nestorians, Indians, Capheturci, Maronites, and very many others of whom it would take long to tell."

As Foucher de Chartres, chaplain to Baldwin and historian of the First Crusade, was to observe, amid this clash of cultures "he who was of the West has become of the East." The European settlers learned Arabic, took Moslem or Eastern Christian women as their brides, followed the example of Baldwin II and grew beards in the Oriental manner, adopted Eastern dress, reclined on carpets to take their meals, and developed a taste for sesame seeds, rice, apricots, melons, Arabic *sukhar* (sugar), *laymun* (lemon), and scallions (the onions of Ashkelon). They grew to appreciate pepper, perfume, incense, carpets, stained glass, the Persian cloth *taftah* (taffeta), and the fabric of Damascus (damask). Advanced Islamic knowledge in such fields as mathematics, medicine, astronomy, and philosophy also found its way to the West.

The central shrine of Christianity, the Church of the Holy Sepulcher, was restored and reconstructed by the Crusaders. It was rivaled as a center of attraction by the Dome of the Rock, for unlike the early Christians, to whom the Temple compound had been a polluted place, the Crusaders had not hesitated to incorporate it into the Christian mysteries. Godfrey of Bouillon, who as *Advocatus Sancti Sepulchri*, Defender of the Holy Sepulcher, briefly held the reins of

authority before the accession of Baldwin I, had granted the Augustinian order some degree of control over the Haram. In time, the friars created a magnificent garden, bordered with a colonnade of marble, as their cloister. It stood opposite the northern entrance to the Templum Domini.

In the transformation of the Dome from Islamic shrine to Christian church, inscriptions in Kufic and Arabic had been plastered over and replaced by bejeweled paintings of Jesus and glittering mosaics depicting events from the Scriptures. Masons carved steps into the rock itself, and an altar was raised atop its pitted surface. Pilgrims clamored for chips of the sacred stone, and the canons, quick to recognize these relics as among the most coveted in Christendom, began trading them for their weight in tithes of gold. Fearing that the rock would disappear, the Latin kings eventually had to order it paved with marble slabs and enclosed within a wrought iron grill to a height "twice that of a man."

The Christians wrought even greater changes upon al-Aksa, the so-called Templum Solomonis. Part served the kings of Jerusalem as a royal residence. The rest was converted into the headquarters and barracks of the proud and aristocratic order of Knights Templar, founded there about twenty years after the conquest.

The colonnaded area that adjoined al-Aksa on the west gave way to the Templars' armory and provision stores, and the vast substructure beneath the mosque, dating back to Herodian times, became a vaulted stable that could easily accommodate four hundred horses. The Franks also incorporated this structure into their intricate tapestry of myth, calling it Solomon's Stables. The name, as well as the vaults themselves, which are supported by a veritable forest of pillars — eighty-eight piers in fifteen rows — survive to this day.

The Templars, resplendent in their armor and mantles of purest white emblazoned with the red cross, became for a time one of the wealthiest and most powerful autonomous organizations in all history. The Templum Domini was both their mother church and the symbol of the order, appearing on the seal of the Grand Master and on their armorial bearings. The polygonal form of the dome influenced the design of the "temple churches" that sprang up in France, Germany, Spain, and England. (The Temple Church of London and the "round churches" of Cambridge, Northampton, and Ludlow Castle were built at this time.) It also appears in Raphael's masterpiece the *Marriage of the Virgin,* which hangs in Milan's Brera Gallery. That a monument distilled of the essence of Islam should become one of the most familiar Christian symbols of medieval Europe is a fascinating bit of irony from a bizarre age.

To Salah al-Din ("Rectitude of Faith") Yusuf ibn Ayub, the Dome of the Rock was far more than a symbol. Its restoration to Islam was the one essential quest of his stormy and spectacular life. A contemporary biographer tells us that Saladin, as the West came to call him, never missed the five daily canonic calls to prayer until the final few days of his life, and that foremost among his entreaties was that he be permitted to live until he had "visited with his own feet the place where the Prophet had set foot, and heard the call from the Rock. . . ."

Two heroic predecessors, Zangi and his son Nureddin, prepared the way for Saladin and the fulfillment of his objective. Aided in part by dissension and jealousy among the Frankish nobles, Zangi, Atabeg of Mosul, recaptured Edessa in 1144. Christendom was in despair. The shock wave rolled across Europe, leading to the launching of the abortive Second Crusade in 1147 under the joint command of France's young king Louis VII and Conrad III of Germany. Like the First, it was decimated by disease and combat en route, and it finally foundered abysmally in a misconceived attempt to capture Damascus the following year.

After Zangi's murder by a demented eunuch in 1146, Nureddin, who was Emir of Aleppo, seized the ring of authority from his father's lifeless fingers and began to systematically reestablish the Moslem union. He annexed Damascus, the last major barrier on the road to Jerusalem. In 1169, after a long and bitter struggle against the enfeebled Fatimid dynasts of Cairo — who had aligned themselves with King Amalric of Jerusalem — Nureddin succeeded in bringing Egypt under his control. This was the turning point in Islam's holy war against the infidel.

The commander of Nureddin's Egyptian campaigns was the portly Shirkuh, whose nephew Saladin served as his chief adviser. When Shirkuh passed away only two months after the victory (not from war wounds but from overeating), it was the thirty-one-year-old Saladin who fell heir to the post of Vizier of Egypt, the richest province in the Moslem world. In May 1174, Nureddin died in Damascus — and through a series of daring political and military maneuvers, Saladin entered Damascus in the autumn as his successor, pro-

claiming himself King of Syria and Egypt.

It took nearly a decade for Saladin to consolidate his position, but in 1183 both Mosul and Aleppo capitulated. The writ of the sultan then ran from the Tigris-Euphrates plain to the shores of North Africa. The very incarnation of the fabled Omar, Saladin presided unchallenged over a new Islamic empire. On the north, east, and south, the borders of the Kingdom of Jerusalem were invested by an adversary who spoke with a single voice. On the west lay the sea.

The ferocity and ambition of al-Malik al-Nasir al-Sultan Saladin, the Victorious King-Sultan, were animated by his abiding faith in the tenets of Moslem orthodoxy, the reawakening of his people, and a burning determination to dislodge the Christian bone in the throat of Islam. But his essential nature was profoundly tempered by an abiding sense of chivalry, gentleness, and humility that rank him as one of the noblest products of high Islamic civilization.

Except when the pressures of combat interfered, Saladin reserved Mondays and Thursdays for public audiences in which he personally dispensed justice and received the petitions of his subjects. He delighted in spending his private hours in intellectual discourse with theologians and scholars.

Tales are legion of the vast amount of personal wealth and booty that the sultan gave away as gifts and acts of charity. He described himself to his personal secretary and biographer Beha ed-Din as a man who "looks on money as one looks on the dust in the road." On one occasion he was forced to cancel a pilgrimage to Mecca because of a "shortage of money necessary to equip himself as became a man of his standing." The estate left by Saladin, a man reckoned as the most powerful of his age, amounted to but forty-seven drachmas and a single piece of Tyrian gold.

If the eventual doom of the Kingdom of Jerusalem could be laid at the doorstep of a single man, it was at that of a reckless Burgundian knight, Reynald de Chatillon, whom the Arabs called Arnat of al-Kerak. His misdeeds left so deep a scar upon Moslem memories that he was singled out in their chronicles as "Islam's most hated enemy." Reynald de Chatillon had marched in the abortive Second Crusade, and with no likelihood of bettering his position at home, he had remained in Palestine. Through marriage, he became Count of Antioch, and later was made lord of Kerak, a great castle on the desolate eastern rim of the Dead Sea, commanding a vital enemy highway.

Unlike the Crusader hierarchy of the first generation, Reynald viewed the Orient less as a home and way of life than as a golden plum to satisfy his adventurous appetite. In 1181 he broke a two-year truce between Saladin and Baldwin IV, the leper king, attacking a richly laden caravan bound for Mecca from Damascus and refusing demands that he compensate Saladin's subjects for the loss of their goods. Reynald then launched a fleet that raided Red Sea ports along the coast of Arabia, seized valuable cargoes from Arab merchant vessels, landed a raiding party that made off with the riches of an Egyptian caravan, and drowned a defenseless shipload of pilgrims who were on their way to Mecca.

Toward the close of 1186, during a second truce and at a time when the shaky kingdom was saddled with the rule of the inept and feeble Guy of Lusignan, Rey-

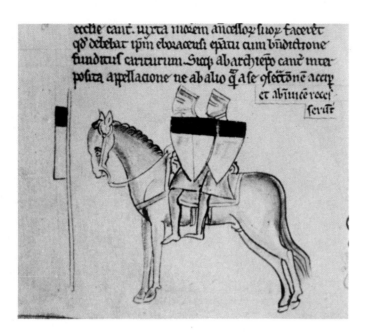

nald committed his final outrage. He ambushed another caravan traveling in the vicinity of Kerak, slaughtering its military escort, making off with his largest haul, and casting the caravaneers into the dungeon of his castle. When they pleaded that he abide by the truce terms, Reynald is said to have replied: "Call on your Mohammed to save you." Saladin, who had once before tried to dispose of the master of Kerak, reacted to the news with cold fury. He made a vow that he would kill Reynald with his own hands.

This was the provocation that drove Saladin to execute final sentence on the nobles of Jerusalem. The following spring he marshaled the largest army he was ever to lead, spearheaded by some 12,000 horsemen. It gathered in the Hauran, behind the basalt hills of Gilead that rise above the Sea of Galilee. In response to the challenge, King Guy raised a force of 1,200 knights and perhaps 18,000 foot soldiers. They gathered at Acre, twenty-five miles due west of Galilee. Reynald and Gerard de Ridfort, Grand Master of the Templars, were among those spoiling for a showdown. The latter was determined to avenge the massacre of ninety of his knights, who had been slaughtered by Al-Afdal, a son of Saladin, during a Moslem reconnaissance in force into Galilee.

On July 1, Saladin's army crossed the Jordan just south of the Sea of Galilee, capturing the ancient town of Tiberias after a brief siege. The Christian forces moved east from Acre and encamped at the spring of Sepphoris. With them was the True Cross, dispatched by Patriarch Heraclius of Jerusalem, who had remained behind, pleading ill health.

The weather was blistering, windless. The grass and thorny scrub blanketing the Galilean hills were scorched to a dead yellow-brown. Count Raymond of Tripoli, whose fief extended to Tiberias, pleaded eloquently against battle, even though his wife was trapped in the beleaguered citadel of the captured town. The defense of the kingdom was their prime purpose, he argued, and the army must remain intact for that purpose. To join battle with Saladin would be suicide. "I prefer to lose my city for a time," he said, "than that the whole country should be lost. Between this place and Tiberias there is not a drop of water. We shall all die of thirst before we get there." King Guy vacillated. But Gerard, who dominated him, would not be put off. "Strike your tents," he urged. "Call the men to arms, and march at once." The king weakly submitted. He would live in guilt and anguish over his folly for the rest of his days.

Saladin had lured the Crusaders into battle on his terms. He held both the western shore of the Sea of Galilee — the only source of fresh water beyond Sepphoris — and the slopes that drop sharply to the lake. Between this escarpment and the Christians lay a rocky, rounded hillock with twin summits called the Horns of Hattin. Here the weary Franks encamped on the night of July 3, 1187, tortured by the heat and, as Raymond had warned, by insufferable thirst. Harassed and weakened by the fast-wheeling skirmishers of the Moslem cavalry, the Crusaders choked on the dust and the acrid smoke of burning brush that the enemy had ignited on the slopes around them. Shimmering tauntingly below was the lake; it would not slake Christian thirst, except perhaps in fevered dreams. The sight drove a few to desert. "Sir," said one of these deserters when he was brought before the sultan, "fall on them

Determined to lift the siege of Tiberias, a Christian fortress on the western shore of the Sea of Galilee, a foolhardy band of Crusaders marched east from their stronghold at Acre — and directly into a trap laid by Saladin. Cut off from their water supply, buffeted by blistering desert winds, and outflanked by the Moslems, the Christians made a desperate, doomed stand on a rubble-strewn plateau known as the field of Hattin (below). Their ranks decimated, the Crusaders withdrew to Jerusalem — and Saladin's armies, fighting one pitched battle after another (right and far right), gradually closed the circle until the Holy City stood alone.

— they cannot help themselves — they are all dead already."

Saladin's forces surrounded the Franks under cover of night, and as the sun rose above the heights of Golan he ordered the attack. Trapped between the savage Moslems and the brush fires, thousands of Christians were cut down as they surged blindly toward the lake. Others, maddened by thirst and exhaustion, threw away their weapons and sat upon the ground, waiting for death. High on Hattin, a ring of 150 knights, shielding the king, the royal tent, and the True Cross, fought desperately on. They absorbed the shock of a Moslem cavalry charge and launched counter-charges, trying to cut through the dense circle of Moslem swords and horsemen that "revolved about them as a globe turns round its pole." The True Cross was lost during the seesaw battle. The enemy pulled the royal tent to the ground, and the exhausted monarch and his surviving bodyguard surrendered.

King Guy and a handful of barons, among them Reynald de Chatillon, were brought before Saladin. Half dead with thirst, Guy begged for a drink and was given a cup of water iced with snow, probably from nearby Mount Hermon. He took a portion and offered the rest to Reynald. Traditionally, hospitality by a Moslem also implies his protection. Angrily, Saladin made it clear that he had not intended his gesture to include Reynald. "Twice I have sworn to kill that man when I had him in my power," he declared. With that, he summoned Reynald before him, raised his sword, and thrust it into the exhausted knight's shoulder. A guard struck off his head. Guy was spared.

So great had been the carnage that bleached bones

still littered the field of Hattin a year later — and only a few knights were available for the defense of Jerusalem. Saladin carefully began to close the net about the city. Within two months, only Tyre, Antioch, Tripoli, Gaza, a handful of castles, and the Holy City remained of the once-proud Christian kingdom. The surrender of Ashkelon on September 4 secured Saladin's communications with Egypt. On that day there was a total eclipse of the sun, a grim omen for the small Christian delegation from Jerusalem that came before the sultan to sue for peace terms that would allow them to retain the city.

"I know that Jerusalem is the House of God," Saladin told them. "I would not willingly assail the House of God, if I can get possession of it by treaty and friendship." He offered them a payment of 30,000 bezants for the city, and promised in exchange a zone of five leagues outside the walls in which they could settle permanently. Alternatively, they could retain possession of Jerusalem until the Pentecost, in the hope of raising an army to defend it. If they failed by that date, they were to peacefully evacuate — "and I will see you all safe and sound on Christian soil."

The delegation refused. They would never willingly abandon the Holy City. Its defense fell upon a noble named Balian of Ibelin, one of the few knights to escape from the field of Hattin. His was a makeshift army of monks, boys, old men, and women. The 20,000 refugees who surged behind Jerusalem's walls at Saladin's approach were of little use. Balian hastily knighted the sons of nobles, the sons of commoners, and thirty burgesses; collected provisions where he could; and stripped gold and silver adornments from the Church of the Holy Sepulcher to be melted into coins to pay his troops.

On September 20, Jerusalem was again at war. For nearly twelve days the city shook under the litany of siege — arrows, Greek fire, the pounding of mangonels and rams. Panic seized the defenders: men deserted the ramparts for the churches to invoke divine aid and confess; monks, priests, and nuns marched in procession chanting the Miserere; and women cut off their daughters' long tresses in an attempt to ward off impending shame. Recalling the terrible carnage eighty-eight years earlier, the besieged expected little better from Saladin — either death, or a lifetime of slavery worse than death.

The Moslems undermined a portion of the northern wall. Their breach was made at the very place where Godfrey of Bouillon had cracked the defenses in 1099, and a large cross erected there to commemorate the event toppled in a cascade of stone and rubble. As a battle raged about the gap, Balian sought an audience with Saladin to sue for humane terms. In desperation, he exploited Saladin's one weakness — his regard for both Jerusalem and his own people. Before the Christians were overcome, Balian vowed, they would see to it that nothing remained for the victors:

We will slaughter our children and our wives. We will burn our possessions so as not to leave you with a dinar or a drachma or a single man or woman to enslave. When this is done, we shall pull down the Sanctuary of the Rock and the Mosque Al-Aksa and other sacred places, slaughtering the Moslem prisoners we hold — 5,000 of them.

Saladin held council with his advisers, and they

quickly agreed that the city must be spared. They told Balian that all Christians would be free to leave Jerusalem in safety upon payment of ransom. Ibn al-Athir tells us that the tax was set at ten gold pieces for each man, five for a woman, two for a child. But Balian objected: the city housed many thousands too poor to pay. A compromise was reached whereby 7,000 of the poor were to be set free for 30,000 dinars, which Balian would raise. He returned to the city and sadly ordered the Christians to lay down their arms.

Subsequently, the compassionate Saladin excluded more than three thousand from the obligation of ransom, together with all the aged. He also promised Christian noblewomen that he would set free those of their husbands whom he held captive, and he even acceded to the plea of Lady Stephanie, widow of the detested Reynald de Chatillon, that her imprisoned son be included.

"The victors were correct and humane," British historian Steven Runciman has written. "Where the Franks . . . had waded through the blood of their victims, not a building now was looted, not a person injured." Saladin's "mercy and kindness were in strange contrast to the deeds of the Christian conquerors of the First Crusade."

It was the period when Moslems celebrate the anniversary of Mohammed's ascent to Heaven from the sacred rock. October 2, 1187, was the day Saladin fulfilled his vow — Holy Friday, his favorite day for war. He entered Jerusalem as endless columns of dispossessed Christians streamed pathetically from the gates, retracing the route of the original Crusaders across a now alien countryside to seek refuge in Christian Tyre.

On that day, the Moslem transformation began. Islamic flags were raised above the city walls. Men clambered atop the dome and took down the gilt cross to repeated shouts of *"Allahu Akhbar"* from Moslem troops below. They dragged the cross through the streets and melted it down as booty. Saladin beamed as he sat in audience outside his pavilion, receiving congratulations from Moslem notables and listening to court poets who declaimed hastily produced panegyrics to the sultan and the victory.

The Dome of the Rock and al-Aksa were thrice cleansed with rose water. Soldiers drafted as workmen removed the plaster hiding the prayer niches that marked the *qibla,* cast out the romanesque statues and sacramental objects, ripped down the mosaic adornments and paintings, stripped away the altar and the marble panels over the sacred rock. They tore down the armory beside al-Aksa, along with the partitions erected within the mosque. The five daily canonic prayers were instituted, and the cries of hastily recruited *muezzins* were soon proclaiming the advent of the new Islamic era of Saladin and his Ayyubid dynasty in Jerusalem.

By the following Friday, October 9, the Haram had been readied for the first observance of the Moslem holy day in nearly a century. Fine rugs, candelabra, copies of the Koran, and prayer mats had been installed in the twin sanctuaries. Saladin himself attended the public service at al-Aksa. "Standards were raised, the pulpit was draped with gorgeous cloths, voices were lifted, groups assembled, throngs crowded together, waves beat upon one another. . . ." The chronicler Imad ad-Din also records that the candidates who vied

for the honor of delivering the first sermon perspired freely awaiting Saladin's choice. It fell upon the chief *qadi* of Damascus, Muhyi ad-Din, who intoned:

> Rejoice at good tidings! God is pleased with what you have done, and this is the summit of man's desires; he hath holpen you to bring back the strayed camel from misguided hands and to restore it to the fold of Islam, after the infidels had mishandled it for nearly a hundred years.

After the service Saladin fulfilled another vow — prostrating himself in prayer in the Dome of the Rock. Then he commanded that both shrines be renewed and gave large endowments for the work. The magnificent cedar pulpit of Nureddin was installed, according to its maker's wish, in al-Aksa mosque. Saladin himself provided a new prayer niche, decorated with marble and mosaic. The mosque and Dome were beautified, and the sultan had the exterior of the Dome's great hemisphere regilded.

Two Christian shrines near the Haram, the Convent of Saint Anne and the Church of Zion, were converted — one into the first of many *madrasahs*, or academies of theology and law, that sprang up on and near the periphery of the sacred compound; the other, into a center of study and meditation for Sufi mystics. Saladin left generous endowments for both while resisting the suggestions of some that the Church of the Holy Sepulcher be demolished. He argued that "it is not the building as it appears . . . but the home of the Cross and the Sepulcher that is the object of worship. The various Christian races would still be making pilgrimages here even if earth had been dug up and thrown into the sky." The tradition of toleration established by Omar ibn al-Khattib would be continued.

The church remained closed for three days before Saladin commanded its reopening for the several thousand Syrian and Armenian Christians who had chosen to remain under his rule. Liberated Moslem prisoners settled in abandoned Frankish houses. To fully repopulate the city the sultan assigned unclaimed houses to clans from selected Arab tribes. He also opened the city to unrestricted Jewish settlement. The new Jewish quarter was established in the southeast quadrant of the city, where it remained until Jordanian times. The first Jewish residents came from Ashkelon. In a short time they were joined by Jews returning from North Africa and as far away as England.

The Christian world had by no means abandoned the Holy Land. Richard the Lion-Hearted assumed the leadership of the Third Crusade, which wrested back the ports of Acre, Jaffa, and Ashkelon but lost its impetus just short of Jerusalem. Like the original Crusaders, Richard caught a glimpse of the walls and towers of the city from the mount of Nabi Samwil, but he hastily shielded his eyes against the sight for he knew the prize would never be his. Even after he exacted from Saladin the right of Christians to make pilgrimage to Jerusalem — a provision of the five-year truce of 1192 — he refused to visit the Holy City.

Early in 1193, Saladin passed away. In 1229, two succeeding monarchs, the Sultan al-Kamil and Emperor Frederick II of Germany, briefly turned back the clock, and the Holy City reverted to Christian rule. But in 1244, warfare again swept the city out of the hands of the West. Jerusalem would not be ruled by Christians again for nearly seven centuries.

VII
Under Mameluke Sway

Many distinctive features of today's Haram took shape during the rule of that uniquely Islamic phenomenon, the Mamelukes. The word "mameluke," which means "one who is owned or possessed," is an appropriate designation for these Turkish-speaking Kurds and Mongols — and Circassians and others from Russia, the Caucasus, and central Asia — for they were originally slaves of the caliphs.

The Abbasids of Baghdad were the first to press the Mamelukes into service as highly reliable bodyguards and fighting troops. Under Saladin's heirs, these alien slave-soldiers had become a privileged caste of military oligarchs — a pivotal center of politics and power in the caliph's court — and it was only a matter of time before the slaves became the masters. On May 2, 1250, as Turanshah, the last of the free Ayyubid dynasts, sat at banquet in Cairo, a Mameluke regiment rose against him. He was chased to the banks of the Nile and hacked to pieces with sabers. The Mameluke commander, a Turk named Izz ad-Din Aybak, was installed as the first Mameluke sultan.

The Mamelukes, who ruled for nearly three centuries, were the last chieftains of the medieval empire of the Arabs and the most feverish of Moslem builders. Never again would architecture flourish as the art of the highest order in Arab lands.

The delicate, arched *mawazeen* that sit athwart the broad staircases of the Dome of the Rock's topmost esplanade date from the Mameluke period, as do the four commanding minarets on the northern and western fringes of the Haram, the shaded colonnades that circumscribe it, and the exuberant masonry of many of the minor domes. Artisans employed by the Mameluke

sultan Tanqiz designed the main *sabil,* the ablutions fountain for worshipers that lies midway between the Dome of the Rock and al-Aksa. Emulating Saladin, who had launched the cultural renaissance over which they presided, the Mameluke sultans also founded and endowed four great religious academies, or *madrasahs,* on the Haram.

Ironically enough, these patrons of Islamic culture were, as a group, coarse and bloodthirsty men. After a reign of only seven years, for example, Sultan Aybak was stabbed to death by eunuchs on the orders of his sultana, Shajar al-Durr, a former Armenian slave who was jealous of his plans to take another wife. Two weeks later, Aybak's outraged harem battered the sultana to death with their wooden shoes and hurled her from a tower. Intrigue and instability haunted the Mamelukes. During their 267-year reign, forty-seven sovereigns sat upon the Mameluke throne — an average tenure of slightly more than five years. In 1421 alone the throne in Cairo changed hands three times.

For the most part, these slave-kings eschewed the principle of hereditary succession; they governed by might, not right. The throne belonged to the strongest, and loyalty was based on bribery and the sword. In this corrupting system lay the seeds of the decline and fall of both the Mamelukes and the territories they controlled, which at one time stretched from Egypt to Palestine, Syria, and the Hejaz. Their failings and excesses — drunkenness, illiteracy, pederasty, insanity — were compounded by famine and plague — which, it is said, eroded the population of Syria, Palestine, and Egypt by two-thirds during this period.

Against this tawdry background the accomplish-

The Damascus Gate, a supreme example of Ottoman architecture, is studded with rosettes like the one at left, each carved with intricate designs.

ments of the Mamelukes seem all the more remarkable. They checked the advance of the Mongol hordes led by Hulagu that might have radically altered both European and Oriental history, and they expelled the last of the Crusaders from the tiny Christian enclaves on the Syrian coast.

It was to the Haram and its precincts that many of the notable Mameluke sultans turned to memorialize their great exploits. It was al-Malik al-Zahir Baybars who crushed the Mongols at the watershed battle of Ain Jalut in Syria in 1260, after they had penetrated as far south as Gaza. And it was Baybars who broke the Crusaders' grip on Nazareth, Caesarea, Arsuf, Safad, Jaffa, Antioch, the fortress of Belfort, and the notorious castle of Kerak in Jordan. In 1270 he renewed the magnificent mosaic decoration in the rotunda of the sacred rock.

The northwest minaret, originally built by the Mameluke Lajin in 1297, was restored three decades later by al-Malik al-Mansur Saif ad-Din Qalawoon. He too scored signal successes against the Mongols, drove the Christians from the vital Syrian port of Tripoli, and launched the siege that led to the fall of Acre, the last anchor of the Latin Kingdom in the East. With its fall, Gibbon wrote, "a mournful and solitary silence prevailed along the coast which had so long resounded with the world's debate."

With Qalawoon's son al-Malik al-Nasir Mohammed, whose reign of forty-two years is the longest in Mameluke annals, Arabic civilization reached its zenith — and began its precipitous fall. Under al-Nasir, the great minaret atop the Gate of the Chain was built. An inscription just above the stained-glass windows in

the Dome of the Rock tells us that he also redecorated the interior with gold and mosaic and added lead shielding to the hemisphere's outer skin in 1448. Shortly thereafter its skeletal timbers caught fire and the dome was seriously damaged despite the fact that "all Jerusalem rushed to save it." Some blamed the tragedy on a thunderbolt; others, on a young boy who had climbed into the dome to hunt pigeons by candlelight. The repairs, undertaken by Az-Zahir Said ad-Din Jaqmaq, required thirty-six tons of lead.

The sultan Barquq (1382–98) presented the magnificent marble pulpit that stands at the southern entrance to the Dome; and Sultan Barsbai (1422–38), who made a habit of beheading physicians who failed to cure him, personally bought a number of villages in Palestine and allotted their revenues to the maintenance of the Haram. The hot-tempered Qaitbay (1468–95), who blinded his alchemist for failing to turn dross into gold, added marvelously wrought copper doors to the Dome of the Rock, and restored the finely executed *sabil*, with its alternating courses of different types of stone, that stands roughly one hundred meters west of the shrine. He also founded the elegant *madrasah* called al-Ashrafiyya.

These were among the last imprints of Mameluke civilization upon the Haram, for the line of semibarbaric slave-warriors had all but burned itself out. Rabbi Obadiah da Bertinoro, who came to Jerusalem in 1488, vividly described the impact of the Mameluke apocalypse on the city: Jerusalem, he wrote, had been shorn of its walls, was "for the most part desolate and in ruins," and contained fewer than four thousand families, only seventy of them Jewish. Most were des-

Interestingly enough, it was the turbulent Mameluke
era — a 267-year period during which some forty-seven
sultans briefly occupied the dynasty's bloodstained throne
— that witnessed the first coordinated renovation of
Jerusalem since Herod's day. On the political front,
successive palace coups exposed the unstable, corrupt,
and highly libidinous nature of these slave-kings. In this
atmosphere of uncertainty the restoration of Jerusalem
took place, beginning with the Dome of the Rock and its
precincts. Four graceful minarets were added to the
corners of the Haram over a period of eighty-nine years,
and it is from these vantages (opposite) that muezzins
raise the traditional Moslem call to prayer. Drawn to the
Haram by this singsong cry, worshipers approach the
Dome itself through a series of tree-shaded colonnades
that were also added by the Mamelukes. The broad
staircases that mark the final ascent to the compound
surrounding the Dome are overarched by Saracenic
arcades known as mawazeen. (In the photograph above,
the delicate arches of a mawazeen frame the northwestern
minaret, which surveys Saint Stephen's Gate.) Among
the projects undertaken by Sultan Qaitbay, whose reign
lasted a remarkable twenty-seven years, was the restoration
of the small sabil, or ablutions fountain, that stands west
of the Dome. A masterpiece of Islamic stonework, that
slender structure (right) is noted for its ingeniously fitted
blocks of variegated stone.

perately poor, underfed, and overtaxed. A dreadful famine had caused widespread mortality, and "many lived on grass, going out like stags to look for pasture." Houses were falling into ruin, and, if their owners were Jewish, could not be rebuilt without the payment of an immense bribe that often cost more than the entire structure was worth.

The energies not only of the Mamelukes but of the Byzantines and Mongols had slackened by the end of the fifteenth century, and circumstances were right for a major realignment of power. The Orient had never been tolerant of weakness; like nature, it abhorred a vacuum. Leadership often passed, as we have seen, to the most unlikely successors, who lurked hungrily on the desolate fringes of the desert and suddenly, as if by magic, acquired the political and military momentum lost by others.

This time, history chose the Ottoman Turks. At the end of the thirteenth century they were little more than a fierce tribe of Turkish-speaking nomads who had wandered west from the steppes of Outer Asia to win a small holding in Anatolia, acquiring the Moslem faith on the way. Their leaders were gifted with intuitive qualities of military discipline and organization, and by the time of the great fire that ravaged the Dome of the Rock in 1448 the dominion of the Ottomans had expanded through conquest to embrace all of Asia Minor, Serbia, Bulgaria, and parts of Albania, Hungary, and Greece. Their crack infantry of Janissaries had repeatedly bested the cream of Europe's armies, and in 1453 the sagacious Turkish sultan Mohammed II had captured the all-but-isolated city of Constantinople, the light of the Christian East, after

a siege of fifty-three days. The Byzantine Empire was no more. Surveying the ancient grandeur of Constantine's splendid city, Mohammed declared: "I have given the captives and the movables to my followers. But the buildings are mine!" The historic capital of Christian Orthodoxy would now become the capital of all Islam under the name Istanbul.

By the summer of 1514 Mohammed II's grandson Selim — who earned the sobriquet "the Terrible" by putting his two elder brothers and eight nephews to death to insure his succession — had forcibly added parts of the Persian Empire to his domain. Two years later, a large but poorly equipped Mameluke army of 80,000 men was routed outside Aleppo by Selim's modern musketry, long-range artillery, mines, and mortars. By 1517, the Ottoman *bunchuk* — the battle standard of horse tails that the Turks had carried into the field since nomadic times — waved from the ramparts of Damascus and Cairo, and the holy cities of Mecca, Medina, and Jerusalem. Selim had become the inheritor of pan-Islamic power, and his domains stretched from the Danube to the Nile, and from the Crimea to the shores of North Africa and the Arabian Peninsula.

When Selim triumphantly entered Jerusalem in January of 1517, the *ulama,* or scholarly council of the city, handed him the keys of the Dome of the Rock and al-Aksa. "Thanks be to Allah," the sultan exclaimed, prostrating himself. "I am now the possessor of the Sanctuary of the First Qibla." A delegation of Christian monks unrolled the scroll of the original writs of Omar, which guaranteed the clerics jurisdiction over the Church of the Holy Sepulcher and the

News of the fall of Constantinople to the Turks was greeted with a mixture of disbelief and dismay in the West, which had long thought of the Eastern Empire as invulnerable. That ominous first blow against the internally corrupt and militarily flaccid dynasties of the Middle East had been struck by Sultan Mohammed II (left), whose grandson Selim was to deliver the final blow at Jerusalem in 1517. A new standard was raised over the city, but not a new religious symbol. Moslems continued to worship at al-Aksa, pausing first to wash their feet in al-Kas, the ablutions fountain built by Sultan Tanqiz (below).

other Christian holy places. These Selim kissed and then confirmed, pressing them to his face and eyes in the Oriental manner. The fate of Jerusalem was sealed for the next four hundred years.

It was not Selim the Terrible who impressed the Ottoman mark upon Jerusalem's stones, for he was to live only three more years — all of which he spent on the battlefield, consolidating his conquests. The chief architect of the modern Haram was Selim's only son, Suleiman — known in the West as "the Magnificent" and in the East as al-Qanuni, "the Lawgiver." It was he who welded the great Ottoman administrative and legal apparatus that governed Arab and Greek, Slav and Turk until the twentieth century.

Yet unlike many of his successors, Suleiman never forgot the sources of Ottoman power. As his legendary grand vizier, Ibrahim, a former Greek slave, once told a European emissary: "Not gold nor gems command; but iron — the sword — by which obedience is assured." Suleiman came to power at the age of twenty-six, an untried ruler in an age of giants — Henry VIII of England, Francis I of France, and Charles V of the House of Habsburg, the powerful Holy Roman Emperor and temporal commander of Western Christendom. Suleiman proved himself more able than any of them. Tall and wiry, thin of face and pallid of complexion, he was greeted with relief by a Europe that had quaked before his father. "A gentle lamb," one Western commentator later reported, "had succeeded a fierce lion."

Rarely in history has there been a deadlier miscalculation — as Europe discovered when Suleiman's land and sea forces succeeded in dislodging the crusading Knights Hospitalers of Saint John from their "impregnable" fortress on the island of Rhodes, then rolled through Belgrade and across Hungary to the very gates of Vienna. Suleiman had gained unchallenged supremacy in the Mediterranean.

Suleiman made Ottoman Turkey the principal factor in European politics in the sixteenth century. In a letter to Francis I, the Commander of the Faithful proclaimed himself to be the "sultan of sultans, the sovereign of sovereigns, the dispenser of crowns to the monarchs on the face of the earth. . . ." And when Charles V described himself in a diplomatic missive as "King of Jerusalem," the vizier Ibrahim could angrily storm at Charles's quavering courier: "Why does he enumerate with such arrogance the titles that are his, and those that are not his? Wherefore does he presume to style himself to my lord as King of Jerusalem? Is he ignorant of the fact that my mighty emperor and not himself, Charles, is Lord of Jerusalem?" Christian Europe came to treat such declarations as anything but bombast.

As a builder, a codifier of Moslem law, a patron of poetry, scholarship, and art, Suleiman was without equal in the history of Islam. In lavishly enriching his empire with public works — schools, hospitals, mosques, fountains, aqueducts, caravanseries, palaces, and public baths — the "Lord of Jerusalem" could scarcely overlook the Holy City itself. In 1537, eight years after the failure of his siege of Vienna and one year after the unprecedented Franco-Turkish entente against the Habsburgs, Suleiman began a campaign to beautify and fortify Jerusalem. One source relates that he financed the project with a thousand purses of gold. His master architect, Sinan, began with the

The Damascus Gate (below, far right), which is Old Jerusalem's principal northern entrance, is one of the best preserved and most original Ottoman structures in the city. Much Turkish architecture of the period is highly derivative, and even the gate — which is considered a prime example of Ottoman art — combines serried arches (near right) and acanthus motifs (far right) that betray Gothic and Grecian antecedents. To stamp the design as their own, Suleiman's architects added bas-relief crescent moons to the lookouts (below, near right).

majestic two-and-a-half-mile circuit of crenellated wall one can still see today. Those pale and massive stones suffuse and absorb the rose tints of dawn, the fiery whites and oranges of midday, the iridescent lavender of sunset, and the deep indigos of Oriental night. The great arched Damascus Gate in the northwestern wall, with its towers and battlements, is a masterpiece of medieval Ottoman art.

Suleiman's artisans repaired and improved the city's water supply, bringing the water from the Pools of Solomon near Bethlehem via a series of aqueducts to feed a complex arrangement of arabesque *sabils* on and about the Haram. They also restored the doors of the Dome of the Rock and added new stained-glass windows of floral design to the mosque.

The sultan's most arresting gift to Jerusalem was a sheath of vibrant tiles for the Dome. The original mosaic exterior had deteriorated during the latter years of the Mameluke period — a result, in all likelihood, of the disappearance of the skilled mosaicists needed to maintain the Dome's decorative covering. Fortunately, Suleiman commanded the talents of the greatest ceramic craftsmen of his age, the tile masters of Kashan in Persia, and he ordered them to provide some 40,000 to 50,000 lustrously painted Kashi tiles as a bold new outer covering for the Dome of the Rock.

What one sees today is a brilliant restoration of those original tiles, which gave the sanctuary a breathless unity of design excelled by few other architectural wonders of man. Their dancing patterns of turquoise, cobalt blue, white, black, brown, and green — coupled with their intricate motifs of quatrefoils, diamonds, stars, stylized leaves and intertwined stems,

lilies and lotuses, and arabesque battlements — seem to challenge the genius of nature itself. Along the parapet of the octagon, in large white letters on a deep blue ground, the thirty-sixth chapter of the Koran has been inscribed. The tile inscription, one of the finest examples of Arab calligraphy, begins: "I swear by the Wise Koran that you are sent upon a straight path. . . ."

Some years after Suleiman's restoration, a Turkish traveler named Evliya Chelebi recorded his rapture upon seeing the Dome: "One is struck dumb at the very sight of it . . . Verily, it is a replica of a heavenly palace. . . . This site stands unique amongst the buildings I have seen, as if it were one of the seven Paradises." Ironically enough, when craftsmen were called upon to reproduce similar tiles for restoration and repair in later ages, they were unable to meet the standards of glazing, draftsmanship, color, and durability established by the men of Kashan in the sixteenth century.

Above the northern portal of the Dome of the Rock, in gold lettering on a plaque of copper, Suleiman, who styled himself "Father of Conquests," commemorated the renovation of "the building which is magnificent and glorious. . . . Thus he has brought to it its ancient glory through the greatest of architects who made it even better than it was." Had the Father of Conquests fully appreciated Jerusalem's checkered history, he might have realized that his boastful pratings would be read by future generations as an epitaph — for the jumbled stones of the Holy City comprise a necropolis for a succession of faded empires. Suleiman's would prove to be no exception.

Indeed, the erosion of Ottoman power began with

Within the octagonal walls of the Dome, concentric rings of marble pillars divide the interior space into three distinct areas. Two ambulatories, both clearly visible in the contemporary photograph below, encircle the central rotunda, which is lit from above by the lunettes that pierce the dome itself.
   Overleaf:
The exterior tiles, the interior giltwork, the luminous stained glass in the gallery — all are beggared when compared with the breathtaking sweep of the dome itself. Here gilt, plaster, and supreme Moslem artistry have combined to produce an extraordinary field of interlocking design and delicate calligraphy.

the ailing sultan's death during a military campaign into Hungary in 1566. The ultimate downfall of the Sublime Porte was postponed for more than four hundred years, however. Moribund for four centuries, "the Sick Man of Europe" at last collapsed in 1917 under the advance of the British Expeditionary Force and its Bedouin allies in World War I.

The vitality of the Ottoman regime had always depended on its elan and momentum as a highly pitched fighting machine — but the constant wars ultimately depleted the energies and resources of the Sublime Porte. In the sixteenth century the Portuguese, Dutch, Spanish, and English came to dominate the lucrative trade routes of the Indian Ocean, the Mediterranean, and the Atlantic Ocean — the routes long dominated by the Turks. Worse still, Turkey had no stake in the New World. Having lost their commercial supremacy, the sultans became helpless witnesses to the collapse of the Turkish economy — and with it, the disintegration of the military and political institutions that had enabled them to govern. The Ottoman frontiers slowly shrank, and the breakdown of central authority led to endemic unrest, mutiny, revolution, widespread corruption by petty officials, and the rise of nationalism among the subject peoples of the empire. The Islamic world was on the wane, and by the time the tottering Ottomans turned to Germany for aid in the Great War, they were ripe for the kill.

Through the centuries of Turkish rule, Jerusalem's fortunes had declined with those of its masters, and by the nineteenth century it was a squalid, provincial, foul-smelling, pestilential Oriental town. There were no roads to speak of. Houses, ill-heated and ill-lit, decayed and crumbled as their owners were driven into poverty by oppressive taxes. The narrow passages of the walled city became receptacles for sewage, rot, and filth; open cesspools bled into water cisterns; and hundreds died of disease each year.

The memoirs of Western travelers who visited the Holy City a century ago reflect a deep sense of disappointment and loss over Jerusalem's fallen state. Lady Judith Montefiore's diary entry in 1885 is typical:

> We are strongly persuaded not to enter the city, cases of plague having occurred within the last few days. . . . The streets were narrow, and almost filled up with loose stones, and the ruins of houses which had fallen to decay. Our guards on each side were busily engaged in keeping off the people, a precaution rendered necessary to lessen the danger of contagion.

In the early 1800's, Jerusalem's population dropped to less than 12,000; Palestine's to only 200,000. Under a subsistence economy further worsened by Ottoman maladministration, farms and villages were neglected or abandoned. The celebrated "land of milk and honey" had reverted to marsh and desert. But events of great moment had begun to intrude upon its slumber.

VIII
Zion Regained

There are many who still vividly recall the historic events surrounding the twenty-third recorded fall of Jerusalem — the defeat of the Turkish army on Nabi Samwil, and the peaceful surrender of the Holy City to the forces of British general Sir Edmund Allenby on December 9, 1917. The proclamation that Allenby issued after his triumphal entry ushered in a new era for Palestine, the Orient, and the West:

> Since your city is regarded with affection by the adherents of three of the great religions of mankind, therefore do I make known to you that every sacred building, monument, holy spot, shrine, traditional site, endowment, pious bequest, or customary place of prayer . . . will be maintained and protected according to the existing customs and beliefs of those to whose faiths they are sacred.

Bells tolled in Jerusalem and in the churches of Great Britain.

In early 1918, a member of the Royal Institute of British Architects named Ernest T. Richmond was hastily summoned to Jerusalem by the Military Governor of the newly established British Occupied Enemy Territory Administration, South. Richmond's assignment was to conduct an emergency study of the parlous condition of the Dome of the Rock.

The structure Richmond found bore little resemblance to the building described by the traveler Chelebi. In the intervening centuries the Dome had become a patched, dilapidated, and weather-beaten testament to the tortuous decline of the Ottoman Empire. The walls of the Dome were mildewed and deteriorating; the great hemisphere was no longer gold but a dull, mottled gray; and its lead sheathing, corroded by age and weather, leaked badly. Marble panels, window frames, and the once-brilliant interior decoration of painted plaster and mosaic were all crumbling at an alarming rate.

After a minute examination of the tile exterior, Richmond concluded that the British and Moslems had an artistic disaster on their hands. The aesthetic concept of the tile masters of ancient Kashan had been lost over the years as the craft of tile-making declined along with Ottoman fortunes. Repairs had been made with inferior tiles of poor durability that warped and cracked in the ovens and faded when exposed to the elements. Man had forgotten the technique by which the Kashi artisans had deftly matched glaze and material to attain the proper coefficient of expansion in firing the tiles.

To make matters worse, this degeneration of the ceramicist's craft was compounded by the makeshift quality of the repairs. At least five renovations were undertaken after Suleiman's time, but for the most part the Ottomans did not renew, but patched. In replacing damaged tiles, they combined a dwindling stock of spares with tiles robbed from other portions of the building. The pieces were chiseled to fit denuded spaces and rearranged on a make-do basis to achieve some sort of crude symmetry. All this, combined with the use of inferior mortar, only hastened the process of weathering. In time, the delicate balance and perfection of the Dome's exterior design vanished — and with it the unity of its eight façades. Toward the end, the Ottoman foremen had pressed into service any material at hand, including common red Marseilles floor tiles. Where mosaic fell away, workmen daubed

For 1,900 years the menorah, or ritual candelabrum, has served Jews as a symbol of both their faith and their lost Temple, demolished by Titus in A.D. 70.

paint over the gaps to simulate the missing pieces.

After months of painstaking scholarship, Richmond completed a "conjectural restoration" of the original Kashi scheme. He then informed his superiors and the Arab elders of Jerusalem that 26,000 new tiles were needed to restore the Dome, and he urged that a school of tile-making be revived in Jerusalem "if the Dome is to live on." Mosaicists also had to be found — if not in the Orient, then in Italy or England.

The Holy City had fallen into such low estate during the years of Ottoman decline that it could scarcely maintain its own shrunken population, let alone an army of skilled craftsmen capable of renovating the Dome of the Rock. Richmond's report underscored the city's bankruptcy, just as his mission dramatized the three pivotal historic developments that had begun to catapult the Holy Land back into the mainstream of world history. These were the "rediscovery" of the Orient by the West after the long cultural and political quarantine that followed the Crusades, the rise of contending empires in Europe whose strategic interests encompassed underdeveloped Asia to the east and Africa to the south, and the arrival in the Middle East of European enlightenment.

Men such as Richmond, the first non-Moslem to gain unrestricted access to the Haram in seven centuries, saw themselves not as conquerors of Palestine but as temporary colonial caretakers acting in the name of civilized society. Theirs was not merely the task of governing the Holy City for a time but of guiding the local Arab, Jewish, and Christian populations in renewing it. Under the League of Nations, Britain held merely a temporary mandate over the Holy Land

— against the day when she would restore it to the peoples whose home it was.

The Jerusalemite scholar Isaac Abbady remembers how British enlisted men, to whom any political sense was alien, "after an exhausting march across the desert," declared to the people who greeted them in the streets of Jerusalem: "We are here to return Palestine to the Jews." The Arabs, who had staked their own dreams for independence from the Turks in particular and foreign domination in general on the long-range goodwill of their British patrons, could only listen silently, filled with vague forebodings of the future.

The incredible rise of Zionism — the revival of nationalist aspirations among the widely scattered descendants of the ancient Israelites — and the tremendous upsurge in Jewish immigration to the Holy Land from the nineteenth century onward stemmed in part from Christian Europe's newfound interest in the area. The man who sparked the European "rediscovery" of the Levant was Napoleon, who had been inspired by a memorandum written by General Leibniz a century before. France, that memorandum suggested, might achieve world supremacy by conquering Egypt. Not only would this give it control of the Old World's strategic center, but it would "also limit and threaten the domination of the English in the Indies."

The thirty-one-year-old Bonaparte had landed in Egypt in 1798 with an army of 40,000 men. His expedition also included a corps of 176 academicians and artists whose mission was to recapture knowledge of the ancient land. A side campaign employing 13,000 troops was launched to seize the port of Acre in Palestine, to protect the French general's eastern flank

Within months of Palestine's liberation by British troops in December 1917, an English architect named Ernest Richmond was called upon to survey the Dome of the Rock, which had fallen into a state of woeful disrepair (right). Richmond's assessment was as disquieting as it was firm: a minimum of 26,000 new tiles would be required immediately if the crumbling structure were to be saved. The results of the ensuing restoration are evident in the exterior recess at left, which encloses a veritable bouquet of assorted floral motifs.

against the Turks in Syria. Harried by the British, Napoleon withdrew from Palestine and, ultimately from Egypt. But the Middle East continued to dominate the thoughts of European empire builders and from that time on France never ceased to play a key role in the affairs of the Orient. The opening of Ferdinand de Lesseps' Suez Canal in 1869 underscored that role.

The first violent explosion among colonial rivals with aspirations in the Middle East was the Crimean War of 1854, ostensibly caused by a dispute concerning jurisdiction over Jerusalem's holy places. In the farsighted view of the Duke of Argyll, writing in 1896, the dream of tsarist Russia was "to make the whole Black Sea a Russian lake, to command the Bosporus and the Dardanelles, and to issue from them into the Mediterranean with fleets powerful in action and inaccessible in retreat." To Britain, the Middle East — with its strategic position and its incomparable naval and communications facilities — became "the ganglion of Empire." Kaiser Wilhelm, on the other hand, envisioned a German empire extending from the North Cape to the Persian Gulf. Oil, first discovered and exploited in Iran at the turn of the century, further whetted the appetites of the West.

In the middle of the nineteenth century energetic exponents of Western enlightenment — antiquarians, scientists, explorers, geographers, and mapmakers — whose curiosity had been aroused by the spectacular discoveries of Napoleon's scholars in Egypt — began to swarm across the face of Palestine and the Orient. Religious scholars and archaeologists, determined to counteract the traumatic impact of Darwinism upon biblical teachings, fought science with science. Founding the study of Palestinology, which sought to establish the "truth" of the Bible, they began to uncover the ruins of many of the lost cities of the Old Testament.

During this period Jerusalem began to rise from the ashes. The United States opened the first diplomatic mission there in 1827, and Britain, France, Prussia, Austria, Spain, and Russia soon followed suit. The seat of the Orthodox patriarchate was moved from Istanbul to Jerusalem and, in 1847, the Latin patriarchate was renewed. In their wake followed a host of state visits by Europe's rising generation of empire builders. One of the first of these was the Prince of Wales, who later became Edward VII of England. In 1855, the Duke of Brabant, the future King Leopold II of Belgium, became the first non-Arab Christian to be escorted through the Dome of the Rock since the expulsion of the Crusaders. Fourteen years later, in honor of the arrival of Emperor Franz Josef of the Austro-Hungarian Empire, the Ottoman sultan built Jerusalem's first modern road, to replace the rutted mule and camel tracks that connected the city with the port of Jaffa forty miles away. In 1898, Sultan Abdul-Hamid II gave the Dome of the Rock a hurried renovation and erected a great Turkish crescent atop it to mark the visit of Kaiser Wilhelm of Germany and his kaiserin, Augusta Victoria.

One of the eyewitnesses to the kaiser's arrival at the Jaffa Gate was a thirty-eight-year-old Viennese journalist named Theodor Herzl, who is known as the father of Zionism. Two years earlier, Herzl had published his epoch-making pamphlet, *The Jewish State;* only months before he had convened the first Zionist

127

Congress at Basel, Switzerland. He had come to Jerusalem to seek the kaiser's support for the Zionists' preeminent goal, a Jewish homeland in Palestine. After the visit Herzl would write:

> If I remember thee, O Jerusalem, in days to come, I shall take little pleasure in the memory. A sink of decay of thousands of years, replete with the corrosion of human life, of black fanaticism hovering like a miasma over its evil-smelling, unclean streets. And should the day come when Jerusalem is once more ours . . . my first act will be to cleanse thee.

For growing numbers of Jews, oppressed by pogroms and segregated in the overcrowded ghettos of Eastern Europe, a vague, two-thousand-year-old dream was suddenly becoming real. Generation after generation had prayed, "If I forget thee, O Jerusalem, let my right hand wither, let my tongue cleave to the roof of my mouth . . . if I set not Jerusalem above my chief joy." Now the promise of Israel was no longer merely a sacred formula to be uttered ritualistically in the synagogue; it was a tangible goal — and a political objective. Some came by ship, others walked overland like the pilgrims of old. They began to pour into Jerusalem, founding a residential settlement just outside the walls, purchasing hopelessly barren countryside tracts from the Arabs, and tilling the land with the aid of donations from brethren abroad. By 1900, Jerusalem had swollen in size to 40,000 — and for the first time since the days of Titus and Hadrian, the majority of its citizens were Jewish. Thirty years later, the Holy City's population was 90,000, of whom 55 per cent were Jewish. A new Jewish city rose west of Suleiman's walls, and during the three decades of the British Mandate the Jewish population of Palestine swelled to over 650,000. It would more than double in the immediate aftermath of the Nazi holocaust in Europe.

The Jewish *Aliyah,* or going up (to Israel), received its first significant assist in 1917, when the Zionist organization in Basel was apprised of a letter written by the British Foreign Secretary, Arthur James Balfour, to Lord Rothschild. It was dated just two days after Allenby launched the campaign that led to Jerusalem's capture, and it read in part: "His Majesty's Government view with favour the establishment in Palestine of a National Home for the Jewish people, and will use their best endeavours to facilitate the achievement of this objective. . . ." To which Balfour added: "Nothing shall be done which may prejudice the civil and religious rights of existing non-Jewish communities in Palestine. . . ."

The British had been caught between two momentous movements — Zionism and awakening Arab nationalism — that were jostling for breathing and living space in the very same territory. The former mayor of Arab Jerusalem, Aref al-Aref, later recalled that the Balfour Declaration took his people completely by surprise. It seemed to run counter to the promises made by London to the old Sherif of Mecca, Hussein ibn-Ali, who had sided with Britain in World War I. (The sherif, who was later known as King Hussein I of the Hejaz, is buried in a tomb in the western cloister of the Haram.) One of the first voices of Arab nationalism to react to the Balfour Declaration was the Commission of the General Syrian Congress, which stated unequivocally on July 2, 1919: "We oppose the pretensions of the Zionists to create a Jewish common-

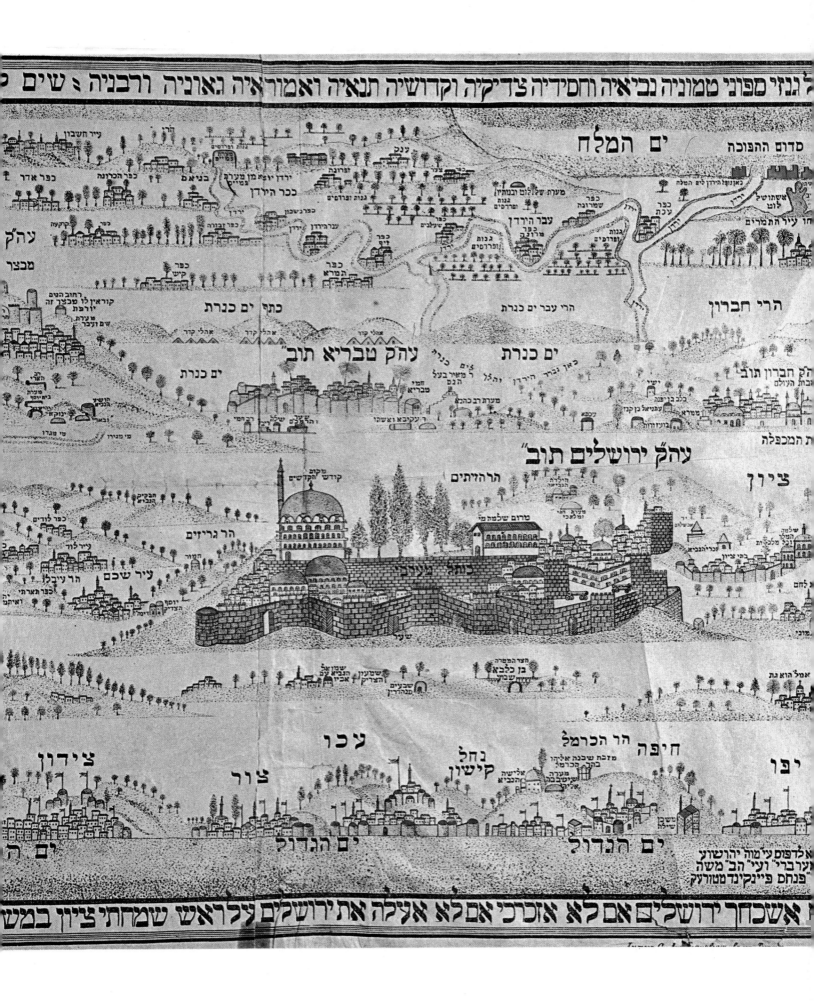

Sir Edmund Allenby and his troops (below) entered liberated Jerusalem in December 1917, two decades after the founding of the Zionist movement and some two weeks after the issuance of the Balfour Declaration. The latter put the British government publicly behind the Zionist cause, a policy shift that was to have a monumental impact upon the modern history of the entire Middle East.

wealth . . . and oppose Zionist migration to any part of our country. . . ."

The seeds of new contention drew sustenance from the dust of the Holy Land, the pulverized residue of the accumulated hates, jostling traditions, conflicting claims, and warring dogmas of ages past. Enmities seemed to flourish in Palestine's soil, but not since the Crusades had the process worked as insidiously as in the confrontation between the Jew — driven from his homeland and fated to spend two thousand years wandering among strangers — and the Arab — subjugated and broken by Turkish overlords. One, the Jew, was rootless and fearful of extinction; the other, the Arab, was self-conscious of his backwardness and seeking an identity lost hundreds of years before. Not even the British, with all their colonial savoir faire and diplomatic skill, could avert the epic confrontation.

The irony of this enduring conflict was never more apparent than in the clash that began at the Wailing Wall, in the shadow of the Dome of the Rock, on September 23, 1928. On that day, the Hebrew Day of Atonement, officials of the Supreme Moslem Council, which administered the Haram and its shrines, complained to British authorities that Jewish preparations for the day of prayer at the Wailing Wall contravened their rights. The Wall, they said, was Moslem property. Religion was not really the issue. The Wall had become an explosive symbol of clashing racial pride and ambition in Jerusalem and Palestine.

Tensions over the Wall intensified the following year, as Moslem leaders inflamed their followers by warning that the Jews wanted nothing less than to seize the Haram, obliterate the Dome of the Rock, and restore the ancient Temple. In the torrid heat of late August 1929, passions overflowed. Jewish worshipers were harassed at the Wall, and during the encounter an aged Jew was hacked to death and another was stabbed. Fifty Jews were killed and a hundred were wounded in a savage massacre at Hebron, and there was a similar outrage at Safad. The Jews fought back, and before British troops and police could quell the outbreak, 250 Jews and Arabs were dead and some 600 were wounded. Similar outbreaks were to continue throughout the 1930's.

World War II magnified the crisis from a struggle between two Semitic peoples into the deadly contest of nations that was to involve virtually the entire globe. Out of a European community of nearly 9,600,000 Jews, whom Hitler set out to systematically eradicate in a campaign of genocide that is without parallel in all of history, some 6,000,000 were to perish by the time Nazi Germany surrendered to the allies in 1945. Thirty thousand survivors were liberated from concentration camps, and another 177,000 fled to Allied displaced-persons camps following fresh persecutions in Eastern Europe. For most of these wretched displaced persons, only Palestine offered a future.

The British guardians of the Holy Land were bedeviled: on the one hand, they were confronted by the rising clamor of Jews demanding permission to migrate from war-torn Europe; and on the other, they were buffeted by the angry objections of the Arab states, which opposed any increase in Palestine's Jewish population. London chose to limit the new Jewish immigration to a trickle — and the Zionist leaders of Palestine, who had all-too-recently suffered the spectacle of European

Jewry's silent submission to decimation by the Nazis, wrathfully embarked on a policy of militant opposition to British policy. The Haganah, an underground militia formed around a nucleus of Jewish veterans of World War II, opened an illegal immigration pipeline from Europe. More extreme elements, such as the Sternists and Irgunists, determined that violence was the only means of carving out a Jewish state, and they began a twilight war of terror against the British in Palestine. The escalating bloodshed eventually prompted London to abandon its thirty-year-old mandate.

On the question of filling the British vacuum, Jews and Arabs were equally polarized. The United Nations therefore resolved upon a plan to partition Palestine between the two, and that scheme was approved in a dramatic General Assembly vote on November 29, 1947. Six months later, on May 14, 1948, as the last of the British withdrew, Israel was reborn after a silence of twenty centuries. The aging Zionist Chaim Weizmann would become its first president; socialist leader David Ben-Gurion, its prime minister.

But the peace for which pilgrims to Jerusalem had so avidly prayed was never to prove more elusive. No sooner had Israel miraculously risen from the dead than the Arabs set out to destroy it. Egyptian planes bombed Tel Aviv as armies from Egypt, Transjordan, Syria, and Lebanon moved across the Israeli frontiers. Some 240,000 Palestinian Arabs in territory assigned to Israel fled to Transjordan, creating the tormenting refugee problem that exists today.

Jerusalem, already scarred from the bombs of the Jewish underground's campaign against the British, underwent the first of two new trials of violence in as many decades. Arab and Jewish armies waged a seesaw war for control of the Holy City, adding a new layer of rubble to the debris of so many centuries. Both the Dome of the Rock and al-Aksa mosque were damaged by bombs and mortars, and when the battle ended inconclusively in an uneasy armistice, the city was artificially divided between Israel and Jordan. The Arabs retained possession of the old walled city, while most of New Jerusalem remained in Israeli hands. Jews were once again denied access to their most sacred shrine, the Wailing Wall.

During the next twenty years, Arab efforts to build a viable union, in emulation of Omar and Saladin, were thwarted by a plague of ideological, political, national, and personal differences. An eminent casualty was King Abdullah of Transjordan, grandfather of Hussein II and one of the most commanding figures in the Arab world. In the aftermath of the 1948 war, he secretly sought to negotiate a permanent peace with Israel while also trying to engineer a union of Lebanon, Jordan, and Iraq. In July of 1951, as he was about to enter al-Aksa mosque for his noon prayers, Abdullah was shot dead by an Arab political assassin recruited by one of the extremist elements in the demimonde of Moslem politics. Even the late, charismatic Gamal Abdel Nasser, who captured the imagination of the Arab masses by overthrowing King Farouk of Egypt in 1952, was unable to knit together a workable pan-Arab coalition.

It was the brief but dramatically decisive Six-Day War of June 1967 that shattered Nasser's pan-Arab dream. That bitter clash secured the hallowed Wailing

Wall for the Jewish state for the first time since A.D. 70, and it earned Israel a preeminence as a Middle Eastern power that it had not known since the days of Solomon. Once again, great armies were deployed along Jerusalem's ancient ramparts — and at 10 A.M. on June 7, Israeli Colonel Mordecai "Motta" Gur gave the signal for the attack on the walled city. Troops of Jordan's Arab Legion stood behind the battlements, just as the Fatimids had in 1099. The Jordanians dug in at the Citadel, where Iftikhar had commanded the Egyptian defense against the Frankish barons, as the ancient stones reverberated once again to the sounds of pitched battle.

Tanks and elements of Gur's reservist paratroop brigade hurled a barrage of artillery fire at the barred portal of Saint Stephen's Gate, just two hundred feet north of the Haram. From his command tank, Gur ordered his driver to speed ahead. They crashed through the gate and quickly reached the Haram, the old Temple Mount. One of Gur's company commanders, Captain Yoram Zamosh, also managed to reach the Haram esplanade. He sped past the Dome of the Rock, clambered to the top of the Wailing Wall, and, oblivious to the battle, draped an Israeli flag from its parapet. "For a while," the Israeli journalist Moshe Brilliant recalls, Zamosh "stood alone, staring open-mouthed at the worn stones with moss growing out of the chinks. . . ." With enemy snipers still firing, the paratroopers dropped their arms, fell before the hallowed Wall or leaned their foreheads against the stones, and burst into racking sobs. The chief military chaplain, Rabbi Shlomo Goren, raced to the Wall carrying the Torah and blowing ritual blasts on a

ram's horn. General Moshe Dayan arrived, wrote the words "May peace come to the Jewish people" on a scrap of paper, folded the sheet, and inserted it into a chink between the stones according to the ancient custom.

A few soldiers would die at the sacred spot before the sniping was stilled. With them died several ecstatic civilians from Israeli Jerusalem, who sped in droves through the narrow passageways of the Old City to the Wall to mark the historic recapture of this sanctified remnant of Titus's destruction. The discontinuity of twenty centuries had been bridged.

The Jordanian governor of the city and the chief *qadi* approached Colonel Gur. Their troops were leaving, they quietly informed him; Arab Jerusalem would not be defended further. Later, officials of the Supreme Moslem Council were reassured that they would remain the sole custodians of the Haram. The Israelis had no claims on the site of their lost Temple except for the Wailing Wall below. Islam's rights to its sacred shrines would be guaranteed by the posterity of Solomon and David.

Today the Dome of the Rock presents one of those intriguing paradoxes that typify Jerusalem's history, for despite the travails of modern Islam, the fabled sanctuary of Abd al-Malik and Suleiman has never been more magnificent. Between 1958 and 1964, independent Arab governments, headed by Egypt, Jordan, and Saudi Arabia, renewed the shrine from foundation to dome at a cost of 750,000 Jordanian dinars. The restoration was total — structural, architectural, and decorative. The artistic conception of Suleiman's Persian tile masters had been revived by the ceramic craftsmen of

Kutahia in Turkey, and the dome's covering, no longer lead but durable anodized gilt aluminum, gleams as it did when first coated with gold by Abd al-Malik. To paraphrase Cardinal Newman's brilliant description of the Bible, the Dome of the Rock is again "like the body of Heaven in its clearness; its variants like the bottom of the sea; its variety like the scenes of nature."

As always, however, Jerusalem remains an uneasy home. Arab claims upon it, pitted against the determination of the Israelis never again to lose their political and spiritual capital, continue to fuel the fires of discord. Once again the words that the Moslem chronicler Ibn Jubair wrote during the turbulent epoch of the Crusades can be applied to the people of the Middle East: "Security never leaves them in any circumstances, neither in peace nor in war."

As in ages past, the essential flaw of human nature condemns the sacred to coexist with the profane in Jerusalem. Thus, on August 21, 1969, a young Australian religious fanatic named Denis Michael Rohan — acting in the name of a "call from on high" to restore the Temple of the Jews — set fire to al-Aska mosque, destroying the incomparable eight-hundred-year-old carved pulpit of Nureddin and Saladin, and inflaming the unstable and distraught Arab world.

Can the Jerusalem of the brilliant Dome, the lost Temple, and the Holy Sepulcher ever be liberated from conflict? After revisiting Jerusalem and the Dome of the Rock in March 1971 the writer could only reflect upon the comment of Samasi, a revered sage of the Islamic Sufis: "Man thinks he is many things. He thinks he is One. He is usually several. Until he *becomes* One, he cannot have a fair idea of what he is at all."

This twelfth-century illumination shows Moslems, Christians, and Jews in Abraham's lap.

JERUSALEM
IN LITERATURE

The Talmud — the extraordinary compilation of the oral law of the Jewish people that supplements and extends the Scriptures — contains a compelling account of the sack of Jerusalem by Nebuchadnezzar, King of Babylon. When the City of David fell in 586 B.C. after a sixteen-month siege, Nebuchadnezzar's armies swept into the fortress for the second time in eleven years. Once again the Babylonians laid waste to the Temple, and once again they carried the Jews into exile. The Book of Lamentations records the sufferings of Nebuchadnezzar's captive "flock" following the capitulation described below.

When the guilt of the Israelites grew too great for the forbearance of the Most High, and they refused to listen to the words and warnings of Jeremiah, the prophet left Jerusalem and travelled to the land of Benjamin. While he was in the holy city, and prayed for mercy on it, it was spared; but while he sojourned in the land of Benjamin, Nebuchadnezzar laid waste the land of Israel, plundered the holy Temple, robbed it of its ornaments, and gave it a prey to the devouring flames. . . .

The followers of Nebuchadnezzar massacred the inhabitants of Jerusalem, the priests and the people, old and young, women, and children who were attending school, even babies in the cradle. The feast of blood at last shocked even the leader of the hostile heathens, who ordered a stay of this wholesale murder. He then removed all the vessels of gold and silver from the Temple, and sent them by his ships, to Babel, after which he set the Temple on fire.

The high priest donned his robe and ephod and saying, "Now that the Temple is destroyed, no priest is needed to officiate," threw himself into the flames and was consumed. When the other priests who were still alive witnessed this action, they took their harps and musical instruments and followed the example of the high priest. Those of the people whom the soldiers had not killed were bound in iron chains, burdened with the spoils of the victors, and carried into captivity. . . .

Thus the people journeyed on with crying and moaning until they reached the rivers of Babylon. Then Nebuchadnezzar said to them, "Sing, ye people, — play for me, — sing the songs ye were wont to sing before your great Lord in Jerusalem."

In answer to this command, the Levites hung their harps upon the willow trees near the banks of the river, as it is written, "Upon the willows in her midst had we hung up our harps." (Ps. 137:2.) Then they said, "If we had but performed the will of God and sung His praises devoutly, we should not have been delivered into thy hands. . . ."

Then said the officers of the captors, "These men are men of death; they refuse to obey the order of the king; let them die."

But forth stepped Pelatya, the son of Yehoyadah, and thus he addressed Nebuchadnezzar.

"Behold, if a flock is delivered into the hands of a shepherd, and a wolf steals a lamb from the flock, tell me, who is responsible to the owner of the lost animal?"

"Surely the shepherd," replied Nebuchadnezzar.

"Then listen to thine own words," replied Pelatya. "God has given Israel into thy hands; to Him art thou responsible for those who are slain."

The king ordered the chains to be removed from the captives, and they were not put to death.

The Talmud

The Pool of Siloam, from a series of nineteenth-century engravings

In the brief space of six years, Judas Maccabaeus profoundly altered the course of Jewish history — and in the process lent his surname to six generations of the Hasmonaean family, whose members are known as the Maccabees. Upon his father's death in 166 B.C., Judas led an avenging army against the Syrians, liberated Jerusalem, and purified the Temple. The warrior-patriot fell in battle during the second Syrian invasion in 160, but his achievements were not forgotten. Hanukkah, the Feast of Dedication, commemorates the resanctification of the Temple; that event is also celebrated in Handel's oratorio Judas Maccabaeus *and Henry Wadsworth Longfellow's verse-drama by the same name. Two scenes from the latter work follow.*

View of Mount Zion

Judas. Who and what are ye, that
    with furtive steps
Steal in among our tents?
    Fugitives. O Maccabaeus,
Outcasts are we, and fugitives as thou art,
Jews of Jerusalem, that have escaped
From the polluted city, and from death.
    Judas. None can escape from death.
      Say that ye come
To die for Israel, and ye are welcome.
What tidings bring ye?
    Fugitives. Tidings of despair.
The Temple is laid waste; the precious
    vessels,
Censers of gold, vials and veils and
    crowns,
And golden ornaments, and hidden
    treasures,
Have all been taken from it, and the
    Gentiles
With revelling and with riot fill its courts,
And dally with harlots in the holy places.
    Judas. All this I knew before.
    Fugitives. Upon the altar
Are things profane, things by the law
    forbidden;
Nor can we keep our Sabbaths or our
    Feasts,
But on the festivals of Dionysus
Must walk in their processions, bearing
    ivy
To crown a drunken god.
    Judas. This too I know.
But tell me of the Jews. How fare the
    Jews?
    Fugitives. The coming of this mischief
      hath been sore
And grievous to the people. All the
    land
Is full of lamentation and of mourning. . . .

The Princes and the Elders
    weep and wail;
The young men and the maidens are
    made feeble;
The beauty of the women hath been
    changed.
    Judas. And are there none to die for
      Israel?
Tis not enough to mourn. Breastplate
    and harness
Are better things than sackcloth. Let
    the women
Lament for Israel; the men should die. . . .
Those of you who are men, put on such
    armor
As ye may find; those of you who are
    women,
Buckle that armor on; and for a watch-
    word
Whisper, or cry aloud, "The Help of God". . . .
    . . . What is peace?
Is it to bow in silence to our victors?
Is it to see our cities sacked and pillaged,
Our people slain, or sold as slaves, or
    fleeing
At night-time by the blaze of burning
    towns;
Jerusalem laid waste: the Holy Temple
Polluted with strange gods? Are these
    things peace?
    Nicanor [commander of a Syrian army
defeated by the Maccabees]. These
are the dire necessities that wait
On war, whose loud and bloody enginery
I seek to stay. Let there be peace
    between
Antiochus [King of Syria] and thee.
    Judas.   Antiochus?
What is Antiochus, that he should prate
Of peace to me, who am a fugitive?
To-day he shall be lifted up; to-morrow
Shall not be found, because he is
    returned
Unto his dust; his thought has come to
    nothing.
There is no peace between us, nor can
    be,
Until this banner floats upon the walls
Of our Jerusalem.

HENRY WADSWORTH LONGFELLOW
Judas Maccabaeus, 1872

THE JEWISH TEMPLE

Joseph ben Matthias, who was born in Jerusalem roughly a decade before Jesus, survived that tumultuous period by compromising the very ideals that doomed the Nazarene. Through a deft combination of flattery and suasion, Joseph managed to convert the surrender of his command post at Jotapata into a stunning personal victory. In capitulating to Vespasian, Joseph emphasized his admiration for the aging field commander, who the defeated Jewish general predicted would be the next Roman emperor. The delighted conqueror subsequently became Joseph's patron, and following the sack of Jerusalem in A.D. 70, the soldier-turned-sycophant accompanied Vespasian's son Titus to Rome. There he adopted the name Flavius Josephus and drafted his twenty-volume history, Antiquities of the Jews. *The following excerpt describes Solomon's splendid Temple, the first major structure to grace the Temple Mount.*

Now, therefore, [Solomon] laid the foundations of the temple very deep in the ground, and the materials were strong stones, and such as would resist the force of time: these were to unite themselves with the earth, and become a basis and a sure foundation for that superstructure which was to be erected over it: they were to be so strong, in order to sustain with ease those vast superstructures, and precious ornaments, whose own weight was to be not less than the weight of those other high and heavy buildings which the king designed to be very ornamental and magnificent. They erected its entire body, quite up to the roof, of white stone: its height was sixty cubits, and its length was the same, and its breadth twenty. There was another building erected over it, equal to it in its measures; so that the entire altitude of the temple was a hundred and twenty cubits. Its front was to the east. As to the porch, they built it before the temple: its length was twenty cubits, and it was so ordered that it might agree with the breadth of the house. . . .

Now the whole structure of the temple was made, with great skill, of polished stones, and those laid together so very harmoniously and smoothly, that there appeared to the spectators no sign of any hammer, or other instrument of architecture, but as if, without any use of them, the entire materials had naturally united themselves together, that the agreement of one part with another seemed rather to have been natural, than to have arisen from the force of tools upon them. The king also had a fine contrivance for an ascent to the upper room over the temple, and that was by steps in the thickness of its wall; for it had no large door on the east end, as the lower house had, but the entrances were by the sides, through very small doors. He also overlaid the temple, both within and without, with boards of cedar, that were kept close together by thick chains, so that this contrivance was in the nature of a support and a strength to the building.

Now when the king had divided the temple into two parts, he made the inner house of twenty cubits [every way], to be the most secret chamber, but he appointed that of forty cubits to be the sanctuary; and when he had cut a door-place out of the wall, he put therein doors of cedar, and overlaid them with a great deal of gold, that had sculptures upon it. He also had veils of blue, and purple, and scarlet, and the brightest and softest of linen, with the most curious flowers wrought upon them, which were to be drawn before those doors. He also dedicated for the most secret place, whose breadth was twenty cubits, and the length the same, two cherubims of solid gold; the height of each of them was five cubits: they had each of them two wings stretched out as far as five cubits; wherefore Solomon set them up

Roman and medieval masonry

not far from each other, that with one wing they might touch the southern wall of the secret place, and with another the northern; their other wings, which joined to each other, were a covering to the ark, which was set between them: but nobody can tell, or even conjecture, what was the shape of these cherubims. He also laid the floor of the temple with plates of gold; and he added doors to the gate of the temple, agreeable to the measure of the height of the wall, but in breadth twenty cubits, and on them he glued gold plates; and, to say all in one word, he left no part of the temple, neither internal nor external, but what was covered with gold.

FLAVIUS JOSEPHUS
Antiquities of the Jews, c. A.D. 70

Like his contemporary John Donne, George Herbert was an ordained minister as well as a practicing poet. Unlike Donne, who preached before heads of state and published voluminously, Herbert remained an unassuming — and unpublished — country cleric all his life. His single volume of collected works, The Temple, *was published posthumously in 1633, shortly after his death and two years after Donne's. The legacy of these metaphysical poets is encapsulated in Herbert's description of the second Temple: "Thy architecture meets with sinne,/ For all Thy frame and fabrick is within."*

Lord, with what glorie wast Thou serv'd of old,
When Solomon's temple stood and flourished!
   Where most things were of purest gold,
   The wood was all embellished
With flowers and carvings mysticall and rare;
All show'd the builders crav'd the seer's care.

Yet all this glorie, all this pomp and state,
Did not affect Thee much, was not Thy aim:
   Something there was that sow'd debate;
   Wherefore Thou quit'st Thy ancient claim,
And now Thy architecture meets with sinne,
For all Thy frame and fabrick is within.

There Thou art struggling with a peevish heart,
Which sometimes crosseth Thee, Thou sometimes it;
   The fight is hard on either part:
   Great God doth fight, He doth submit.
All Solomon's sea of brasse and world of stone
Is not so deare to Thee as one good grone [groan].

And truly brasse and stones are heavie things —
Tombes for the dead, not temples fit for Thee;
   But grones are quick, and full of wings,
   And all their motions upward be;
And ever as they mount like larks they sing;
The note is sad, yet musick for a king.

GEORGE HERBERT
The Temple, 1633

Napoleon's Egyptian Expedition of 1798–99 was, simultaneously, a strategic failure and an archaeological triumph — for during the brief period that the general's troops held the Nile valley, French scientists unearthed the Rosetta Stone. The discovery of that slab of basalt, the key to deciphering Pharaonic hieroglyphs, touched off an era of intensive exploration in the Middle East. By 1895, the year that Thomas Hardy finished Jude the Obscure, *that rediscovery was in full bloom — and it is therefore entirely appropriate that Hardy has built a scene around an elaborate scale model of ancient Jerusalem.*

For a few weeks their work had gone on with a monotony which in itself was a delight to him. Then it happened that the children were to be taken to Christminster to see an itinerant exhibition, in the shape of a model of Jerusalem, to which schools were admitted at a penny a head in the interests of education. They marched along the road two and two, she beside her class with her simple cotton sunshade, her little thumb cocked up against its stem; and Phillotson behind, in his long dangling coat, handling his walking-stick genteelly, in the musing mood which had come over him since her arrival. The afternoon was one of sun and dust, and when they entered the exhibition-room few people were present but themselves.

The model of the ancient city stood in the middle of the apartment, and the proprietor, with a fine religious philanthropy written on his features, walked round it with a pointer in his hand, showing the young people the various quarters and places known to them by name from reading their Bibles: Mount Moriah, the Valley of Jehoshaphat, the City of Zion, the walls and the gates, outside one of which there was a large mound like a tumulus, and on the mound a little white cross. The spot, he said, was Calvary.

"I think," said Sue to the school-master, as she stood with him a little in the background, "that this model, elaborate as it is, is a very imaginary production. How does anybody know that Jerusalem was like this in the time of Christ? I am sure this man doesn't."

"It is made after the best conjectural maps, based on actual visits to the city as it now exists."

"I fancy we have had enough of Jerusalem," she said, "considering we are not descended from the Jews. There was nothing first-rate about the place, or people, after all — as there was about Athens, Rome, Alexandria, and other old cities."

"But, my dear girl, consider what it is to us!"

She was silent, for she was easily repressed; and then perceived behind the group of children clustered round the model a young man in a white flannel jacket, his form being bent so low in his intent inspection of the Valley of Jehoshaphat that he was almost hidden from view by the Mount of Olives. "Look at your cousin Jude," continued the school-master. "He doesn't think we have had enough of Jerusalem!"

"Ah — I didn't see him!" she cried, in her quick light voice. "Jude — how seriously you are going into it!"

Jude started up from his reverie, and saw her. "Oh — Sue!" he said, with a glad flush of embarrassment. "These are your school-children, of course! I saw that schools were admitted in the afternoons, and thought you might come; but I got so deeply interested that I didn't remember where I was. How it carries one back, doesn't it? I could examine it for hours, but I have only a few minutes, unfortunately, for I am in the middle of a job out here."

"Your cousin is so terribly clever that she criticises it unmercifully," said Phillotson, with good-humored satire. "She is quite sceptical as to its correctness."

"No, Mr. Phillotson, I am not — altogether! I hate to be what is called a clever girl — there are too many of that sort now!" answered Sue, sensitively. "I only meant — I don't know what I meant — except that it was what you don't understand!"

"*I* know your meaning," said Jude, ardently (although he did not). "And I think you are quite right."

"That's a good Jude — I know *you* believe in me!" She impulsively seized his hand, and leaving a reproachful look on the school-master turned away to Jude, her voice revealing a tremor which she herself felt to be absurdly uncalled for by sarcasm so gentle. She had not the least conception how the hearts of the twain went out to her at this momentary revelation of feeling, and what a complication she was building up thereby in the futures of both.

The model wore too much of an educational aspect for the children not to tire of it soon, and a little later in the afternoon they were all marched back to Lumsdon, Jude returning to his work. He watched the juvenile flock, in their clean frocks and pinafores, filing down the street towards the country beside Phillotson and Sue, and a sad, dissatisfied sense of being out of the scheme of the latters' lives had possession of him. Phillotson had invited him to walk out and see them on Friday evening, when there would be no lessons to give to Sue, and Jude had eagerly promised to avail himself of the opportunity.

Meanwhile the scholars and teachers moved homeward, and the next day, on looking on the black-board in Sue's class, Phillotson was surprised to find upon it, skilfully drawn in chalk, a perspective view of Jerusalem, with every building shown in its place.

"I thought you took no interest in the model, and hardly looked at it?" he said.

"I hardly did," she said, "but I remembered that much of it."

THOMAS HARDY
Jude the Obscure, 1895

THE CITADEL UNDER SIEGE

Perhaps the most vivid and certainly the most dispassionate account of the sack of Jerusalem in A.D. 70 is the one written by first-century Rome's preeminent historian, Cornelius Tacitus. Writing only a few decades after the city's capitulation, Tacitus was able to assess the tragedy in human as well as historical terms. Thus, for example, Titus is depicted as restless on the eve of battle — eager to complete the conquest and return to Rome, whose many splendors flit before his eyes. Auguries — an integral part of pagan cosmology — are also present.

The Jews formed in order of battle under the very walls, determined, if successful, to push forward; and, if obliged to give ground, secure of a retreat. The cavalry, with the light-armed cohorts, sent against them, fought with doubtful success. Soon the enemy gave way, and on the following days engaged in frequent skirmishes before the gates, till at length, after a series of losses, they were forced to retire within the walls. The Romans resolved now to carry the place by storm. To linger before it till famine compelled a surrender, appeared indeed unworthy of them, and the soldiers demanded the post of danger, some from courage, many from hardihood and the hope of gaining rewards. Rome, her splendours and her pleasures, kept flitting before the eyes of Titus himself; and if Jerusalem did not fall at once, he looked upon it as obstructing his enjoyments. But Jerusalem, standing upon an eminence, naturally difficult of approach, was rendered still more impregnable by redoubts and bulwarks by which even places on a level plain would have been competently fortified. Two hills that rose to a prodigious height were enclosed by walls constructed so as in some places to project in angles, in others to curve inwards. In consequence the flanks of the besiegers were exposed to the enemy's weapons. The extremities of the rock were abrupt and craggy; and the towers were built, upon the mountain, sixty feet high; in the low ground, a hundred and twenty feet. These works presented a spectacle altogether astonishing. To the distant eye they seemed to be of equal elevation. Within the city there were other fortifications enclosing the palace of the kings, and the tower of Antonia, with its conspicuous pinnacles, so called by Herod, in honour of Mark Antony.

Gihon Spring

The Temple itself was in the nature of a citadel, enclosed in walls of its own, and more elaborate and massy than the rest. The very porticoes that surrounded it were a capital defence. A perennial spring supplied the place with water. Subterraneous caverns were scooped out in the mountains, and there were basins and tanks as reservoirs of rain-water. It was foreseen by the founders of the city, that the manners and institutions of the nation, so repugnant to the rest of mankind, would be productive of frequent wars; hence every kind of provision against a siege, howsoever protracted; and exposed as they had been to the successful assault of Pompey, their fears and experience had taught them many expedients. On the other hand, having purchased the privilege of raising fortifications through the venality of the Claudian times, they constructed such walls in a period of peace as showed they had an eye to war; while their numbers were augmented by a conflux of people from every quarter. . . .

Suddenly the portals of the sanctuary were flung wide open, and a voice, in more than mortal accents, was heard to announce that the gods were going forth; at the same time, a prodigious bustle, as of persons taking their departure: occurrences which few interpreted as indicative of impending woe: the majority were deeply impressed with a persuasion that it was contained in the ancient writings of the priests, that it would come to pass at that very time, that the East would renew its strength, and they that should go forth from Judaea should be rulers of the world. Mysterious words, which foreshowed Vespasian and Titus: but the people, according to the usual course of human fondness, interpreting this consummation of destiny as referring to themselves, were not induced to abandon their error even by affliction. We learn that the number of the besieged of every age, male and female, was six hundred thousand; all that were capable bore arms, and more than could be expected out of that number had the fortitude to do so. The devotion of the women was equal to that of the men; and if they must needs move their seat, and quit the habitation of their fathers, they dreaded to live more than to die. Such was the city, such the nation, against which Titus Caesar determined to act.

CORNELIUS TACITUS
Histories, A.D. 109

Rallied by Pope Urban II and led by Godfrey of Bouillon, the soldiers of the First Crusade launched an all-out assault upon the heavily fortified, Turkish-held citadel of Jerusalem in 1099. The ensuing battle, which the renowned English historian Edward Gibbon describes in detail in the following excerpt from his massive Decline and Fall of the Roman Empire, *resulted in a massacre of unparalleled dimensions. Gibbon's account concludes with an extraordinary* tableau vivant: *the "bloody victors," contrite in triumph, ascend Calvary to pray at the Church of the Holy Sepulcher, "monument of their redemption."*

Godfrey of Bouillon erected his standard on the first swell of Mount Calvary: to the left, as far as St. Stephen's gate, the line of attack was continued by Tancred and the two Roberts; and Count Raymond established his quarters from the citadel to the foot of Mount Sion, which was no longer included within the precincts of the city. On the fifth day, the crusaders made a general assault, in the fanatic hope of battering down the walls without engines, and of scaling them without ladders. By the dint of brutal force, they burst the first barrier; but they were driven back with shame and slaughter to the camp: the influence of vision and prophecy was deadened by the too frequent abuse of those pious stratagems; and time and labor were found to be the only means of victory. The time of the siege was indeed fulfilled in forty days, but they were forty days of calamity and anguish. A repetition of the old complaint of famine may be imputed in some degree to the voracious or disorderly appetite of the Franks; but the stony soil of Jerusalem is almost destitute of water; the scanty springs and hasty torrents were dry in the summer season; nor was the thirst of the besiegers relieved, as in the city, by the artificial supply of cisterns and aqueducts. The circumjacent country is equally destitute of trees for the uses of shade or building; but some large beams were discovered in a cave by the crusaders: a wood near Sichem, the enchanted grove of Tasso, was cut down: the necessary timber was transported to the camp by the vigor and dexterity of Tancred; and the engines were framed by some Genoese artists, who had fortunately landed in the harbor of Jaffa. Two movable turrets were constructed at the expense, and in the stations, of the duke of Lorraine and the count of Tholouse, and rolled forwards with devout labor, not to the most accessible, but to the most neglected, parts of the fortification. Raymond's Tower was reduced to ashes by the fire of the besieged, but his colleague was more vigilant and successful; the enemies were driven by his archers from the rampart; the draw-bridge was let down; and on a Friday, at three in the afternoon, the day and hour of the Passion, Godfrey of Bouillon stood victorious on the walls of Jerusalem. His example was followed on every side by the emulation of valor; and about four hundred and sixty years after the conquest of Omar, the holy city was rescued from the Mahometan yoke. In the pillage of public and private wealth, the adventurers had agreed to respect the exclusive property of the first occupant; and the spoils of the great mosque, seventy lamps and massy vases of gold and silver, rewarded the diligence, and displayed the generosity, of Tancred. A bloody sacrifice was offered by his mistaken votaries to the God of the Christians: resistance might provoke, but neither age nor sex could mollify, their implacable rage: they indulged themselves three days in a promiscuous massacre; and the infection of the dead bodies produced an epidemical disease. After seventy thousand Moslems had been put to the sword, and the harmless Jews had been burnt in their synagogue, they could still reserve a multitude of captives, whom interest or lassitude persuaded them to spare. Of these savage heroes of the cross, Tancred alone betrayed some sentiments of compassion; yet we may praise the more selfish lenity of Raymond, who granted a capitulation and safe-conduct to the garrison of the citadel. The holy sepulchre was now free; and the bloody victors prepared to accomplish their vow. Bareheaded and barefoot, with contrite hearts, and in an humble posture, they ascended the hill of Calvary, amidst the loud anthems of the clergy; kissed the stone which had covered the Savior of the world; and bedewed with tears of joy and penitence the monument of their redemption.

EDWARD GIBBON
Decline and Fall of the Roman Empire, 1788

THE PILGRIM TRAIL

Nineteen years after the conquest of Jerusalem by the Christians in 1099, the Knights Templar founded their order on the site of the al-Aksa mosque — a few yards south of the Dome of the Rock itself. By the middle of the twelfth century, the Franks had eased their original restrictions on Moslem worship sufficiently to permit visitors such as Usamah Ibn Munqidh to pray in al-Aksa. Harassment of the faithful and intolerance of religious diversity remained a fact of life, however, as Ibn Munqidh rather testily records.

A proof of the harshness of the Franks (the scourge of Allah upon them!) is to be seen in what happened to me when I visited Jerusalem. I went into the mosque Al-Aksâ. By the side of this was a little mosque which the Franks had converted into a church. When I went into the mosque Al-Aksâ, which was occupied by the Templars, who were my friends, they assigned me this little mosque in which to say my prayers. One day I went into it and glorified Allâh. I was engrossed in my praying when one of the Franks rushed at me, seized me and turned my face to the East, saying, "That is how to pray!" A party of Templars made for him, seized his person and ejected him. I returned to my prayers. The same man, escaping their attention, made for me again and turned my face round to the East, repeating, "That is how to pray!" The Templars again made for him and ejected him, then they apologised to me and said to me, "He is a stranger who has only recently arrived from Frankish lands. He has never seen anyone praying without turning to the East". I answered, "I have prayed sufficiently for to-day". I . . . was astounded to see how put out this demon was, how he trembled and how deeply he had been affected by seeing anyone pray in the direction of the *Kibla.*

I saw one of the Templars go up to the emir Mou'în ad-Dîn (may Allah have mercy upon him!) when he was in the cathedral of the Rock (*As-Sakhra*). "Would you like", he asked him, "to see God as a child?" "Yes, certainly", answered Mou'în ad-Dîn. The Templar went before us until he showed us an image of Mary with the Messiah as a child (may he be saved!) on her lap. "Here", said the Templar, "is God as a child." May Allâh raise himself high above those who speak such impious things!

The Franks understand neither the feeling of honour nor the nature of jealousy. If one of them is walking with his wife and he meets another man, the latter takes the woman's hand and goes and talks to her. . . .

USAMAH IBN MUNQIDH
Autobiography, c. 1150

The natural ebullience and heightened sensitivity that made Alphonse de Lamartine one of the most influential forces in the Romantic movement in nineteenth-century France give his prose a buoyancy and verve that seem all but irrepressible. Lamartine was known in his own time as an orator as well as a poet, and both talents are clearly displayed in his stirring and evangelical account of his 1832 pilgrimage to the Holy Land. In the following passage, Lamartine lauds King David, whom he calls "the sweet singer of Israel! the first poet of sentiment!"

This is Sion! the palace, the tomb of David! the seat of his inspiration and of his joys, of his life and his repose! A spot doubly sacred to me, who have so often felt my heart touched, and my thoughts rapt by the sweet singer of Israel! the first poet of sentiment! the king of lyrics. Never have human fibres vibrated to harmonies so deep, so penetrating, so solemn. Never has the imagination of a poet been set so high, never has its expression been so true. Never has the soul of man expanded itself before man and before God, in tones and sentiments so tender, so sympathetic, and so heartfelt! All the most secret murmurs of the human heart found their voice, and their note, on the lips and the harp of this minstrel! And if we revert to the remote period when such chants were first echoed on the earth; if we consider that at the same period the lyric poetry of the most cultivated nations sang only of wine, love, war, and the victories of the muses, or of the coursers at the Eleian games, we dwell with profound astonishment on the mystic accents of the prophet-king, who addresses God the Creator, as friend talks to friend; comprehends and adores His wonders, admires His judgments, implores His mercies, and seems to be an anticipatory echo of the evangelic poetry, repeating the mild accents of Christ before they had been heard. Prophet or not, as he is contemplated by the philosopher or the Christian, neither of them can deny the poet-king an inspiration bestowed on no other man! Read Horace or Pindar after a psalm? — For my part I cannot!

I, the feeble poet of an age of silence and decay, had I domesticated at Jerusalem, should have selected for my residence and abiding place, precisely the spot which David chose for his at Sion. Here is the most beautiful view in all Judea, Palestine or Galilee. To the left lies Jerusalem with its Temple and its edifices, over which the eyes of the king or of the poet might rove at large without his being seen from thence. Before him, fertile gardens descending in steep declivities, lead to the bed of that torrent, in the roar and foam of which he delights. Lower down, the valley opens and extends itself; fig-trees, pomegranates, and olives over-shadowing it. On one of these rocks suspended over the rolling tide; in one of these sonorous grottoes, refreshed by the breeze and by the murmur of the waters; or at the foot of a trebinthus, ancestor of that which shelters me, the divine poet doubtless awaited those inspirations which he so melodiously poured forth! And why will they not here also visit me, that I might recount in song the griefs of my heart, and of the hearts of all men, in these days of perplexity, even as he sang of his hopes in an era of youth and of faith? Song, alas! no longer survives in the heart of man, for despair sings not! And until some new beam shall descend upon the obscurity of our times, terrestrial lyres will remain mute, and mankind will pass in silence from one abyss of doubt to another, having neither loved, nor prayed, nor sang.

ALPHONSE DE LAMARTINE
A Pilgrimage to the Holy Land, 1832

Church of the Holy Sepulcher

The Haram Ash-Sharif

Outraged over the unjust seizure and arbitrary execution of one of his colleagues, French author and statesman François René de Chateaubriand resigned his post in Napoleon's government in 1804 and went into self-imposed exile. The log of his travels includes this description of Jerusalem's "mosque of the Rock."

Titus having taken Jerusalem in the second year of Vespasian's reign, not one stone was left upon another of that Temple where Christ had done such glorious things, and the destruction of which he had predicted. When Omar took Jerusalem, it appears that the site of the Temple, with the exception of a very small part, had been abandoned by the Christians. Said-Eban Batrik, an Arabic historian, relates that the caliph applied to the patriarch Sophronius, and enquired of him what would be the most proper place at Jerusalem for building a mosque. Sophronius conducted him to the ruins of Solomon's Temple.

Omar, delighted with the opportunity of erecting a mosque on so celebrated a spot, caused the ground to be cleared, and the earth to be removed from a large rock where God is said to have conversed with Jacob. From that rock the new mosque took its name of Gameat-el-Sakhra, and became almost as sacred an object to the Mussulmans as the mosques of Mecca and Medina. The caliph Abd-el-Malek made additions to its buildings, and enclosed the rock with walls. His successor, the caliph El Oulid, contributed still more to the embellishment of El·Sakhra, and covered it with a dome of copper, gilt, taken from a church at Balbek. In the sequel, the Crusaders converted the Temple of Mahomet into a sanctuary of Christ; but when Saladin retook Jerusalem, he restored this edifice to its original use.

But of what nature is the architecture of this mosque, the type, or primitive model, of the elegant architecture of the Moors? This is a question which is very difficult to resolve. The Arabs, in consequence of their despotic and jealous habits, have reserved their decorations for the interior of their monuments; and the penalty of death was denounced against every Christian who should not only enter the Gameat-el-Sakhra, but merely set foot in the court by which it is surrounded. It is much to be regretted, that Deshayes, the ambassador, out of a vain diplomatic scruple, refused to see this mosque, into which the Turks offered to introduce him. I shall describe the exterior as it appeared to me, and give such particulars of the interior as we have learned from various travellers and historians.

The great square of the mosque, formerly the great square of the Temple, may be seen from a window in Pilate's house. This square forms a court, about five hundred paces in length, and four hundred and sixty in breadth. On the east and south this court is bounded by the wall of the city, on the west by Turkish houses, and on the north by the ruins of the Praetorium of Pilate and Herod's palace.

Twelve porticoes, placed at unequal distances, and perfectly irregular, like the cloisters of the Alhambra, form the entrances [to the great square]. . . .

In the midst of this court is a smaller, raised like a terrace, without balustrade, six or seven feet above the former. This second court is, according to the general opinion, two hundred paces long and one hundred and fifty broad. . . .

In the centre of this upper court stands the famous mosque of the Rock. Close to the mosque is a cistern, which receives its water from the ancient *Fons Signatus*, and at which the Turks perform their ablutions before they go to prayer. Some aged olive-trees and cypresses are thinly scattered over both courts.

The temple itself is an octagon: a lantern, which has likewise eight sides and a window in each, crowns the edifice. This lantern is covered with a dome, formerly of copper guilt, but now of lead: a pinnacle, in a very good style, terminated by a crescent, rises at the top of the whole structure, which resembles an Arabian tent pitched in the middle of a desert. Father Roger gives thirty-two paces for the measure of each side of the octagon, two hundred and fifty-two for the external circumference of the mosque, and eighteen or twenty fathoms for the total height of the building.

The walls are lined externally with small tiles or bricks, painted with different colours: these bricks are covered with arabesques, and verses from the Koran, inscribed in letters of gold. The eight windows of the lantern are adorned with circular panes of stained glass. Here we already discover some original features of the Moorish edifices in Spain: the light porticoes of the court, and the painted bricks of the mosque, remind you of different parts of the Generalif, the Alhambra, and the cathedral of Cordova.

Let us now proceed to the interior of this mosque, which I have not seen, and which it was impossible for me to see. I was strongly tempted to run every risk in order to gratify my love of the arts; but was deterred by the fear of involving all the Christians at Jerusalem in destruction.

The most ancient author that has described the mosque of the Rock is William of Tyre, who could not fail to be well acquainted with it, since it had but just been wrested out of the hands of the Christians at the period when the sagacious archbishop wrote his history. He speaks of it in the following terms:

"We have said, at the beginning of this book, that Omar, the son of Caled, erected this temple; a circumstance which is evidently proved by the ancient inscriptions engraven both within and without this edifice." The historian then proceeds to the description of the court, and adds: "In the angles of this court were extremely lofty towers, from the top of which the priests of the Saracens were accustomed at certain hours to summon the people to prayers. Some of these towers remain standing to this day, but the others have been destroyed by various accidents. No person was allowed to enter or remain in this court otherwise than with his feet uncovered and washed.

"The temple is built in the middle of the upper court; it is octagonal, and adorned both internally and externally with squares of marble and mosaic work. The two courts, both the upper and the lower, are paved with white flag-stones to catch in winter the rain-water, which falls in great abundance from the buildings of the temple, and runs very clear, and without any mixture of mud, into the cisterns below. In the middle of the temple, between the inner range of columns, is a rock of no great height, and at the foot of it is a grotto hewn out of the same stone. Upon this rock sat the angel, who, as a punishment for David's inconsiderate numbering of the people, slaughtered them till God commanded him to return his sword into the scabbard. This rock, previously to the arrival of our armies, was naked and uncovered, and in this state it remained for fifteen years; but those to whose care this place was afterwards entrusted covered it again, and erected upon it a chapel and an altar for the performance of divine worship."

FRANCOIS RENÉ DE CHATEAUBRIAND
Travels to Jerusalem and the Holy Land, 1804

WORSHIPERS AT THE HARAM ASH-SHARIF

Just as Lamartine and Chateaubriand celebrated Jerusalem's Christian heritage, so Arab visitors extolled the city's Moslem shrines. One in particular praised the Holy City with such unwavering fervor that he came to be known as al-Muqaddasi the Jerusalemite.

The Kâdi Abu'l Kâsim, son of the Kâdi of the Two Holy Cities [Mecca and Medina], inquired of me once concerning the climate of Jerusalem. I answered, "It is betwixt and between — neither very hot nor very cold." Said he in reply, "Just as is that of Paradise." The buildings of the Holy City are of stone, and you will find nowhere finer or more solid constructions. In no place will you meet with a people more chaste. Provisions are most excellent here, the markets are clean, the mosque is of the largest, and nowhere are Holy Places more numerous. The grapes are enormous, and there are no quinces to equal those of the Holy City. In Jerusalem are all manner of learned men and doctors, and for this reason the hearts of men of intelligence yearn towards her. All the year round, never are her streets empty of strangers. Now one day at Busrah I was seated in the assembly of the Chief Kâdi Abu Yahya ibn Bahrâm, and the conversation turned on the city of Cairo. Then one said, speaking to me, "And can any city be more illustrious?" I replied, "Why, yes, my own native town!" Said he, "But is any pleasanter than Caro?" I answered, "Yes again, my native town." It was said, "Ah, but Cairo is the more excellent; and the more beautiful; and the more productive of good things, and the more spacious." Still, to each and all I replied, "Not so! it is my native town." Then the company were astonished, and they said to me, "Thou art a man of erudition, but thou dost advance now more than can be accorded to thee, in our belief. . . ." So I answered them and spake: "Now, as to my saying that Jerusalem is the most illustrious of cities, why is she not one that unites the advantages of This World to those of the Next? He who is of the sons of This World and yet is ardent in the matters of the Next, may with advantage seek her markets; while he who would be of the men of the Next World, though his soul clings to the good things of This, he, too, may find these here! And as to Jerusalem being the pleasantest of places in the way of climate, why the cold there does not injure, and the heat is not noxious. And as to her being the finest city, why, has any seen elsewhere buildings finer, or cleaner, or a mosque that is more beautiful? And as for the Holy City being the most productive of all places in good things, why Allah — may He be exalted — has gathered together here all the fruits of the lowlands, and of the plains, and of the hill country, even all those of the most opposite kinds; such as the orange and the almond, the date and the nut, the fig and the banana. . . . And as to the excellence of the City! why, is not this to be the plain of marshalling on the Day of Judgment; where the gathering together and the appointment will take place? Verily Makkah and Al Madinah [Mecca and Medina] have their superiority by reason of the Ka'abah and the Prophet — the blessing of Allah be upon him and his family — but verily, on the Day of Judgment, they will both come to Jerusalem, and the excellences of them all will there be united. And as to Jerusalem being the most spacious of cities; why, since all created things are to assemble there, what place on the earth can be more extensive than this!"

AL-MUQADDASI
Description of Syria, Including Palestine, 985 A.D.

Although her description of Jerusalem in 1905 focuses upon what she calls the strangest, saddest, and most moving sight on earth — the assembling of the city's Jews at the Wailing Wall on Sabbath eve — Matilde Serao also comments extensively on the "Mosque of Omar," which looms above the Wall. In her tempered treatment of both faiths and both shrines, the Italian novelist captures the polytheistic essence of modern Jerusalem.

The Wailing Wall

Every Friday a procession of Christians, starting from the Praetorium, passes through the streets of Jerusalem, kneeling and praying at every one of the fourteen "stations," and thereby performing what is known as the "Way of the Cross." At each "station" they recall the heartrending episode it records; the fateful dialogue between Pontius Pilate and the surging mob of angry Jews, "What then shall I do with Jesus which is called Christ?" And they answering said, "His blood be on us and on our children." When Pilate again exclaimed: "I am innocent of the blood of this just person." And thus is fulfilled every Friday throughout the year this Jewish imprecation with deepest and saddest testimony. By a strange coincidence, too, on Fridays, the Jews who inhabit Jerusalem, about thirty thousand in number, close their shops and places of business, lock up their dwellings and quit their malodorous quarters, and the city, except in the Christian districts, is deserted. The markets are closed: the last camels, with empty sacks across their humps, have gone home towards Bethlehem, Jericho, or St. John-of-the-Mountain. The ancient Solima, the city of David and Solomon, is wrapped in silence: the breath of Israel seems to have swepts its streets: the small Nazarene quarter, that of Jesus, is entirely overrun by the Jews in the performance of their rites. Whither have the pale-faced, thin, violet-lipped, the sad, proud-eyed people of Zion fled? The Christians returning from the Via Dolorosa regain their hotels or the Franciscan convent, to rest after their exciting pilgrimage of the "Way of the Cross.'" Later in the afternoon they are reminded by their faithful guides that they should go and witness the most pathetic of sights, the "Wailing of the Jews." Every Friday the Jewish population . . . abandons business and trade to give vent to its pent-up feelings by weeping and wailing before the walls of its erstwhile time-honoured Temple. There is no stranger, sadder, or more moving sight on earth than this weekly "Wailing of the Jews" of Jerusalem.

A wall! Not an ordinary wall, but a lofty, overpowering mass of Cyclopean brickwork: is all that now remains of the Temple of Solomon; of the Seat of the Mosaic Law; of that Temple whose grandeur and majesty fills the Scriptures. Only a wall — but so magnificent, so colossal, that the sonorous descriptions of it do not appear exaggerated; and the eye raised to take in its height is quickly lowered, as if humbled by the spectacle of so much might and strength. The stones of which the wall of the Temple is made are long, wide, and thick, and are more like huge slabs, evenly placed one above the other, forming a sheer rock, square, polished, heavy, and overwhelmingly strong. All else has been demolished: did not Jeus say that He could destroy the Temple and build it up again in three days? Nothing remains of its rich inlaid woods, ivories, and precious stones, which made it so bewilderingly bright and lovely: only this wall is left standing to show what the Temple must have been, and the power of the Hand which crumbled it to dust. These huge slabs alone bear witness to the past glory of Israel, and, in order that the curse might seem the more tragic, Fate has

decreed that this wall, which testifies to the greatness of Moses and Solomon, to the pride and splendour of a nation, should now be the support of the left wing of the Mosque of Omar!

The Turks, during the reign of Omar, made use of the foundations of the Temple to build a magnificent mosque, the most important in Islam, after the one at Mecca, which contains the Prophet's tomb, and that of Medina. The wall, which was covered with costly woods, carbuncles, and emeralds, and inlaid work of gold and copper: the sacred wall which had witnessed the solemn rites of the Law of Moses has now become the prop of a mosque, whose only ornaments are straggling Mohammedan inscriptions and a series of blue and yellow tiles running along the great cornice of its interior. The wall looks on to a narrow, dirty alley, where its huge grey stones contrast strangely with the neighbouring small houses and squalid huts. The glory of Solomon has vanished; the greatness of the Jewish people is no more; that sacred wall which heard the Judaic prophecies and prayers, which was the ideal cradle of the Law, is now polluted by Mohammedans. The Jews who come every Friday to wail and weep, never enter the Mosque of Omar, which they hold in horror, for it is said that the Book of the Law was buried underneath the peristyle, and they fear to enter lest they might, inadvertently, tread it under their feet. They cannot, moreover, bear to see the Crescent shining over the place where the Ark of the Covenant once was venerated; or to see the *mirhab* on the site of the Tabernacle. Every Friday, women, children, old men and young, set out for the narrow lane where King Solomon's mighty wall still endures. The women wear a kind of toque of silk or wool over their hair, and above it a light woollen shawl with a flowery pattern, in the folds of which they hide half their faces. The Russian and Polish Jews wear a fur cap; others, the French and English, a black silk cap; and some still wear the real old Hebrew *Zimarra*. Along the houses opposite the wall of Solomon there are stones and benches upon which the old people and children sit, praying and reading their holy books. And all along the wall itself, with their foreheads pressed against it, is a crowd of women, their shawls thrown back from their heads, with shoulders bent, weeping in silence; and thus the cold, smooth, wall gradually becomes saturated with tears. Two or three hundred people at a time, men and women, congregate there, remaining ten minutes or a quarter of an hour, sobbing silently. When they have finished their wail, two or three hundred other people take their places, beating their heads against the stone, praying and weeping; and as they do so they recite in a dismal monotone, a doleful yet touching litany that begins thus: —

"For our destroyed Temple — Here we come and weep.
For our fallen glory — Here we come and weep.
For our exterminated people — Here we come and weep."

The rabbi . . . says the first part of this dreary dirge, to which the mourning people make answer. And as the narrative of their misfortunes continues and all the fulness of the misery of the Jewish race, with no fatherland, no nationality, and no king, is unrolled in one great lamentation, the wailing increases.

MATHILDE SERAO
In the Country of Jesus, 1905

155

The publication of The Jewish State *in 1896 inaugurated the modern Zionist era and propelled its author, a Hungarian-born journalist named Theodor Herzl, from relative obscurity to international prominence. Six years later the father of Zionism completed an equally visionary work in an altogether different mode. Herzl's* Old-New Land, *a quasi-autobiographical exercise in futuristic fiction, describes the "cooperative society" the author envisioned for the new Jewish state. The novel is unabashed propaganda, and it is also a rather transparent roman à clef: Kingscourt is a German misanthrope whom Herzl almost certainly drew from life, and Friedrich Loewenberg is none other than Herzl himself. In the excerpt below, the two men enter a gleaming Jerusalem whose skyline includes a Peace Palace, symbol of Herzl's unfulfilled dream for the strife-torn city.*

Twenty years before, Kingscourt and Friedrich had entered Jerusalem by night and from the west. Now they came by day, approaching from the east. Then she had been a gloomy, dilapidated city; now she was risen in splendor, youthful, alert, risen from death to life.

They came directly from Jericho up to the top of the Mount of Olives with its wide views. Jerusalem and her hills were still sacred to all mankind, still bore the tokens of reverence bestowed upon her through the ages. But something had been added: new, vigorous, joyous life. The Old City within the walls, as far as they could see from the mountain top, had altered least. The Holy Sepulcher, the Mosque of Omar, and other domes and towers had remained the same; but many splendid new structures had been added. That magnificent new edifice was the Peace Palace. A vast calm brooded over the Old City.

. . . the Old City . . . lay in the afternoon sunlight, on the farther side of the Kidron Valley. . . . Kingscourt had put all sorts of questions, and David had answered them all. Now he asked, What was that wonderful structure of white and gold, whose roof rested on a whole forest of marble columns with gilt capitals? Friedrich's heart stirred within him as David replied, "That is the Temple!"

Friedrich's first visit to the Temple was on a Friday evening. David had engaged rooms for the party at one of the best hotels near the Jaffa Gate, and at sundown invited his guests to go with him to the Temple. . . . Throngs of worshipers wended their way to the Temple and to the many synagogues in the Old City and the New, there to pray to the God Whose banner Israel had borne throughout the world for thousands of years.

The spell of the Sabbath was over the Holy City, now freed from the filth, noise and vile odors that had so often revolted devout pilgrims of all creeds when, after long and trying journeys, they reached their goal. In the old days they had had to endure many disgusting sights before they could reach their shrines. All was different now. There were no longer private dwellings in the Old City; the lanes and the streets were beautifully paved and cared for. All the buildings were devoted to religious and benevolent purposes — hospices for pilgrims of all denominations. Moslem, Jewish, and Christian welfare institutions, hospitals, clinics stood side by side. In the middle of a great square was the splendid Peace Palace, where international congresses of peace-lovers and scientists were held, for Jerusalem was now a home for all the best strivings of the human spirit: for Faith, Love, Knowledge.

THEODOR HERZL
Old-New Land, 1902

Gilbert Keith Chesterton, the English essayist, novelist, poet, and critic, wrote
The New Jerusalem *at roughly the midpoint in his prolific career. In such lines
as "it is my fixed intention to call it the Mosque of Omar, and with ever renewed
pertinacity to continue calling it the Mosque of Omar" Chesterton reveals a
fractiousness that both enlivens and emboldens an otherwise scholarly commen-
tary on the city and the Dome. The following excerpt also reflects the welling
fascination with the Christian mysteries that was to lead to Chesterton's conversion
to Catholicism in 1922, a year after* The New Jerusalem *was issued.*

There is no better way to get a preliminary plan of the city than to follow
the wall and fix the gates in the memory. Suppose, for instance, that a man
begins in the south with the Zion Gate, which bears the ancient name of
Jerusalem. This, to begin with, will sharpen the medieval and even the
Western impression first because it is here that he has the strongest sentiment
of threading the narrow passages of a great castle; but also because the very
name of the gate was given to this south-western hill by Godfrey and Tancred
during the period of the Latin kingdom. I believe it is one of the problems
of the scholars why the Latin conquerors called this hill the Zion Hill, when
the other is obviously the sacred hill. Jerusalem is traditionally divided into
four hills, but for practical purposes into two; the lower eastern hill where
stood the Temple, and now stands the great Mosque, and the western where
is the citadel and the Zion Gate to the south of it. I know nothing of such
questions; and I attach no importance to the notion that has crossed my own
mind, and which I only mention in passing, for I have no doubt there are a
hundred objections to it. But it is known that Zion or Sion was the old name
of the place before it was stormed by David; and even afterwards the Jebusites remained on this western hill, and some compromise seems to have been
made with them. Is it conceivable, I wonder, that even in the twelfth century
there lingered some local memory of what had once been a way of distinguish-
ing Sion of the Jebusites from Salem of the Jews? The Zion Gate, however, is
only a starting-point here; if we go south-eastward from it we descend a steep
and rocky path, from which can be caught the first and finest vision of what
stands on the other hill to the east. The great Mosque of Omar stands up
like a peacock, lustrous with mosaics that are like plumes of blue and green.

Scholars, I may say here, object to calling it the Mosque of Omar; on the
petty and pedantic ground that it is not a mosque and was not built by Omar.
But it is my fixed intention to call it the Mosque of Omar, and with ever
renewed pertinacity to continue calling it the Mosque of Omar. I possess a
special permit from the Grand Mufti to call it the Mosque of Omar. He is
the head of the whole Moslem religion, and if he does not know, who does?
He told me, in the beautiful French which matches his beautiful manners,
that it really is not so ridiculous after all to call the place the Mosque of
Omar, since the great Caliph desired and even designed such a building,
though he did not build it. I suppose it is rather as if Solomon's Temple had
been called David's Temple. Omar was a great man and the Mosque was a
great work, and the two were telescoped together by the excellent common
sense of vulgar tradition. There could not be a better example of that great
truth for all travellers; that popular tradition is never so right as when it is
wrong; and that pedantry is never so wrong as when it is right. And as for
the other objection, that the Dome of the Rock (to give it its other name) is
not actually used as a Mosque, I answer that Westminster Abbey is not used

The Mount of Olives from Jerusalem

as an Abbey. But modern Englishmen would be much surprised if I were to refer to it as Westminster Church; to say nothing of the many modern Englishmen for whom it would be more suitable to call it Westminster Museum. And for whatever purposes the Moslems may actually use their great and glorious sanctuary, at least they have not allowed it to become the private house of a particular rich man. And that is what we have suffered to happen, if not to Westminster Abbey, at least to Welbeck Abbey.

The Mosque of Omar (I repeat firmly) stands on the great eastern plateau in place of the Temple; and the wall that runs round to it on the south side of the city contains only the Dung Gate, on which the fancy need not linger. All along outside this wall the ground falls away into the southern valley; and upon the dreary and stony steep opposite is the place called Acaldama. Wall and valley turn together round the corner of the great temple platform, and confronting the eastern wall, across the ravine, is the mighty wall of the Mount of Olives. On this side there are several gates now blocked up, of which the most famous, the Golden Gate, carries in its very uselessness a testimony to the fallen warriors of the cross. For there is a strange Moslem legend that through this gate, so solemnly sealed up, shall ride the Christian King who shall again rule in Jerusalem. In the middle of the square enclosure rises the great dark Dome of the Rock.

GILBERT KEITH CHESTERTON
The New Jerusalem, 1921

Political turmoil has been endemic in the Holy Land for millennia, and much of that strife has focused upon the walled city of Jerusalem. In 1967, the struggle for possession of the city and its shrines took a dramatic and seemingly decisive turn when an Israeli army detachment stormed the Old City and seized the ancient Temple Mount. The noted American military historian S. L. A. Marshall interviewed the participants for this account.

The night of 6–7 June in Jerusalem was made for forays, alarms, and confusions. Amitai's troops that had taken Government House went way out to capture Deir Agu Tor, a Jordanian village overlooking the Holy City. At 1830, [Colonel Mordecai] Gur's brigade started on the second phase, the capture of the eastern hills. After taking all day to refit, the tanks showed up at 1900, and it was already dark. Gur led them to the wall, where he pointed the way. One company under Captain Aitan was to provide a covering fire for the attack by the second battalion; the other was to advance directly against Augusta Victoria, the battalion objective.

In the dark, Captain Raffi [the tank commander] lost his way, made the wrong turn, got on the main road to Jericho, and ran into intense artillery fire. He called on radio to Gur: "Somehow I've missed; tell me where I am." Gur asked him: "What do you see around you?" Raffi read off the signs. Gur, a Jerusalem-born Sabra who knew the city like his own backyard, recognized nothing. He could not imagine that Raffi had strayed so far afield.

Gur dispatched Major Capusta of the reconnaissance unit to look for Raffi. Capusta scouted forward for a distance, then returned to instruct one of his platoon commanders how to proceed with the search. The unit set forth. Minutes passed. Gur heard cries on his radio: "Doctor, doctor, please doctor." It was the voice of the platoon commander. For better or worse,

Jerusalem from the Mount of Olives

he too had missed the turn, wheeled onto the Jericho road, come under heavy fire from the wall, and gotten himself, his people, and his jeeps well riddled.

Out of the second error, Gur at last understood what had happened. He told his G-2 (intelligence officer), Major Arik: "Go to the Jericho road and bring back Raffi's tanks." His G-3 (staff officer for operations), Major Amos, was told to take Aitan's company and replace Raffi's company for the assault on Augusta Victoria hill. The second battalion under Ouzi was ordered to proceed with the mission.

All this was in vain. Gur started toward the scene of the impending action. On his way he heard from General Narkis on radio that a strong force of Jordanian armor (forty Pattons) was coming along the Jericho road; Gur's entire brigade should fold back into a defensive position.

. . . Jordan's Pattons were indeed coming on. Figuring Gur's people were too worn down to brace against tanks, Narkis asked for an air strike on the Jericho road. The planes came over, dropped many flares, then reported that they had hit and stopped the armor. It was another mistake of the night. They had strafed, instead, a battalion of 25-pounder artillery. But indirectly the air strike had done its work. Wanting none of it, the armor turned about. By that time the tanks of Ben-Ari's brigade were already threatening Jericho through the back door.

At 0500 on 7 June, Narkis got this word from the high command: "You must move as quickly as possible and take the Old City. A cease-fire is coming fast."

The message altered all calculations. Narkis had set 1100 as the time for the operation he had discussed with [General Moshe] Dayan the day before. He now brought it forward two hours. At 0830 Wednesday the air force put a telling strike on the main target. At 0900 Gur's troops captured Izaria and at 0945, they broke through St. Stephen's Gate (also called the Lion's Gate). Gur was first in his half-track. Ten minutes later they had arrived at the Dome of the Rock.

At 1010, Narkis, moving in his own half-track, joined Gur at the Wailing Wall. What great words are said by simple soldiers in such high moments? Narkis remarked: "It's fantastic." Gur answered: "To be here, yes." There were about two hundred troops with Gur at the Wall, and fire from snipers was kicking up dirt and bouncing from the rock all about.

Fighting on quite a different line, the Jerusalem brigade was at the same time occupying the ground from Mount Zion to the east for one-half mile, to assist the advance of Gur's forces. . . . By 1030 one of Gur's battalions was at the Mosque of Omar. Shortly after noon, all Jerusalem was under Israel's control. Soon after 1600, Amitai's brigade turned toward Bethlehem and Hebron, taking off from Ramat Rahael. Bethlehem was taken just before sundown; there had been little resistance along the road. No fire was directed against the city of Christ's birth and none came forth.

There are few scars from the fighting, on either the Old City or the New. By the hour of the cease-fire, when all of the West Bank was in Israel's hands, most of the rubble had been cleared from the Jerusalem streets, and the wire barricades and mine fields were fast disappearing. Of the two brigades, one hundred twenty-five men had died to make the city whole again.

S. L. A. MARSHALL
Swift Sword, 1967

REFERENCE

Chronology

Entries in boldface refer to the Temple Mount and the Dome of the Rock.

c. 2000 B.C.	Abraham enters Jerusalem
c. 1200	Moses leads Israelites from Egypt; his followers, led by Joshua, arrive in Canaan
c. 996	David wrests Jerusalem from the Jebusites
c. 970	Solomon succeeds David as King of Israel
c. 950	**First Temple completed**
721	Sargon II of Assyria conquers northern Israel
587–86	Nebuchadnezzar of Babylon invests, and ultimately conquers Jerusalem; **Temple destroyed**
539	Cyrus of Persia topples Babylonian Empire; Jerusalem freed
520	**Zerubbabel, a descendant of the House of David, begins rebuilding Temple**
515	**Rebuilt Temple inaugurated**
169	Antiochus IV, Seleucid King of Palestine, marches on Jerusalem to impose conformity of worship; **Temple pillaged**
167	**Temple again defiled by Antiochus's soldiers**
164	**Maccabees drive Seleucids from the Temple compound**
63	Pompey conquers Jerusalem
39	Herod elected King of the Jews
31	Mark Antony, Herod's patron, defeated by Octavian at Actium
20	**Construction of Herod's Temple begun**
c. 4	Birth of Jesus; death of Herod
c. A.D. 29	Trial, persecution, and crucifixion of Jesus
66	**Gessius Florus's troops loot Temple treasury, slaughtering worshipers and rabbis**
70	**Titus captures, sacks, and razes second Temple**
132–35	**Last Jewish revolt suppressed by Hadrian, who obliterates Temple and city of Jerusalem**
324	Constantine the Great unites Eastern and Western Roman empires
325	Constantine calls Council of Nicaea; city of Jerusalem rededicated
c. 325	Constantine's mother, Helena, makes pilgrimage to Palestine, where she discovers the True Cross and selects the sites of the Church of the Holy Sepulcher and the Church of the Nativity
333	Bordeaux Pilgrim reaches Jerusalem
410	Rome sacked by the Goths; many Roman aristocrats take refuge in Jerusalem
570	Birth of Mohammed
614	Sassanid Persians put Jerusalem to the torch
622	Mohammed's Hegira to Medina
629	Emperor Heraclius liberates Jerusalem
630	Mohammed's 10,000-man army marches on Mecca
632	Death of Mohammed
637	**Arabs capture Jerusalem; Omar builds first mosque on site of second Temple**
670	**Bishop Arculfus writes first description of Omar's mosque**
687	**Abd al-Malik begins replacing mosque with Dome of the Rock**
691	**Dome of the Rock completed**
1054	As East-West schism widens, pope excommunicates patriarch of Constantinople
1077	Seljuk Turks seize Jerusalem from the Fatimids
1088	Urban II elected pope
1093	Peter the Hermit joins pilgrim caravan bound for Jerusalem
1095	At Council of Clermont, Urban II calls for a Crusade to reclaim the Holy Land
1096	First Crusade departs for the Holy Land
1098	Crusaders take Antioch; Fatimids recapture Jerusalem from the Seljuk Turks
1099	Crusaders capture Jerusalem, butchering its defenders and inhabitants
1100–18	Reign of Baldwin I, first ruler of the Kingdom of Jerusalem
1118	**Order of the Knights Templar establishes its headquarters in the al-Aksa mosque**
1124	Baldwin II eliminates taxes on imports and allows Moslem merchants to market their wares in Jerusalem once again.
1140	**Relaxation of restrictions permits Arabs to visit the Dome of the Rock**
1144	Zangi recaptures Edessa from Crusaders, touching off Second Crusade (in 1147)

1146	Zangi assassinated; his son and successor, Nureddin, orders Arab craftsmen to fashion a cedar pulpit to be installed in al-Aksa upon its liberation by the Moslems
1169	Nureddin subdues Egypt
1174	Nureddin dies and is succeeded by Saladin
1181	Reynald de Chatillon, "Islam's most hated enemy," breaks uneasy two-year truce between Moslems and Crusaders
1186	Second truce ends when Reynald attacks a caravan of pilgrims bound for Mecca; Saladin declares *jihad,* or holy war, against the infidel
1187	Saladin captures Jerusalem
1192	Saladin and Richard the Lion-hearted sign a five-year truce ending the Third Crusade
1193	Death of Saladin
1229	Jerusalem briefly reverts to Christian rule under Frederick II of Germany
1244	Jerusalem recaptured by the Arabs
1250	Mamelukes rise against the Ayyubid caliphs in Cairo, beginning 267-year reign
1260	Baybars, fourth Mameluke sultan, crushes Mongols in battle of Ain Jalut
1270	**Baybars restores the mosaic rotunda of the Dome of the Rock**
1297	**Mameluke Lajin adds northwest minaret to the Haram**
c. 1390	**Sultan Barquq adds marble pulpit to the southern entrance to the Dome**
1448	Under Mohammed II, Arabic civilization reaches its zenith; **minaret added to Gate of the Chain, interior mosaics and outer lead sheath added to Dome of the Rock; fire damages Dome**
1453	Mohammed II successfully besieges the city of Constantinople
1517	Mohammed's grandson Selim captures Jerusalem
1537	Suleiman the Magnificent begins campaign to beautify and fortify Jerusalem, beginning with the city's perimeter walls and the huge Damascus Gate; **new stained-glass windows added to Dome of the Rock; doors restored; exterior sheathed in vibrant tiles**
1566	Death of Suleiman
1827	United States opens first diplomatic mission in Jerusalem
1847	Latin patriarchate in Jerusalem renewed
1854	Crimean War fought by Turkey, England, France, and Russia — ostensibly to settle the question of jurisdiction over Jerusalem's holy sites
1855	**Duke of Brabant becomes first non-Arab to tour Dome since expulsion of the Crusaders**
1896	Theodor Herzl publishes *The Jewish State;* First Zionist Congress convened in Basel
1917	Allenby enters Jerusalem; surrender of the Ottoman army to the British; Balfour Declaration puts Great Britain on record as favoring "a National home for the Jewish people"
1918	**Ernest T. Richmond surveys Dome, recommends immediate action to save deteriorating façade and interior**
1919	Syrian congress declares itself opposed to further Zionist migration
1929	Savage attacks on Jews in Jerusalem, Hebron, and Safad rekindle religious antagonism
1945	Germany surrenders; 30,000 Jews liberated from Nazi concentration camps
1946	Haganah, nationalist underground organization, opens illegal immigration pipeline to Israel
1947	United Nations votes partition of Palestine
1948	British withdraw from Palestine; war engulfs region; **Dome and al-Aksa damaged by bombs**
1951	**King Abdullah of Transjordan, early advocate of Arab confederation, assassinated in al-Aksa**
1956	Anglo-French forces invade Suez
1958–64	**Egypt, Jordan, and Saudi Arabia underwrite extensive repairs of the Dome**
1967	Six-Day War: Israelis wrest Golan Heights, Sinai, Gaza, and the west bank of the Jordan from the Arabs; Old Jerusalem seized; **Wailing Wall and Haram liberated**
1969	**Denis Michael Rohan, an Australian religious fanatic, sets al-Aksa afire, destroying the pulpit of Nureddin**

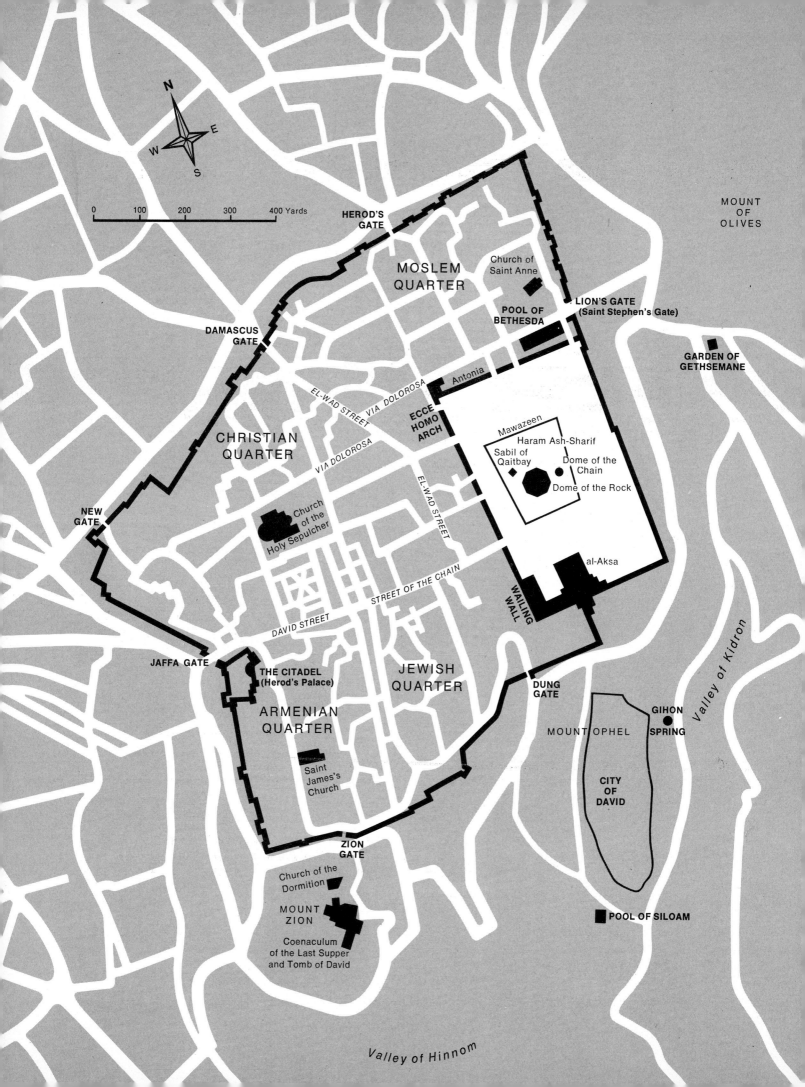

N

W E

S

0   100   200   300   400 Yards

HEROD'S GATE

MOSLEM QUARTER

Church of Saint Anne

POOL OF BETHESDA

LION'S GATE (Saint Stephen's Gate)

DAMASCUS GATE

MOUNT OF OLIVES

GARDEN OF GETHSEMANE

EL-WAD STREET

VIA DOLOROSA

Antonia

VIA DOLOROSA

ECCE HOMO ARCH

CHRISTIAN QUARTER

Mawazeen

Haram Ash-Sharif

Sabil of Qaitbay

Dome of the Chain

Dome of the Rock

EL-WAD STREET

NEW GATE

Church of the Holy Sepulcher

al-Aksa

STREET OF THE CHAIN

WAILING WALL

JAFFA GATE

DAVID STREET

JEWISH QUARTER

THE CITADEL (Herod's Palace)

DUNG GATE

Valley of Kidron

ARMENIAN QUARTER

MOUNT OPHEL

GIHON SPRING

Saint James's Church

CITY OF DAVID

ZION GATE

Church of the Dormition

MOUNT ZION

Coenaculum of the Last Supper and Tomb of David

POOL OF SILOAM

Valley of Hinnom

Guide to Old Jerusalem

Old Jerusalem is a uniquely endowed city. An ancient Hebrew saying attempts to account for the turns of fate that have afflicted the city by noting: "When God created beauty, He created ten parts of it and gave nine to Jerusalem; when He created knowledge, He did the same; and the same when He created suffering."

The city is revered as the birthplace of the world's three great monotheistic religions — Judaism, Christianity, and Islam. Ignoring the political disputes that threaten its peace, thousands of visitors — tourists and religious pilgrims — come to Jerusalem each year to walk its thickly populated streets and rediscover the fountainhead of Western man's spiritual heritage.

Modern Jerusalem is actually three cities in one: the largely Jewish New Jerusalem, capital of Israel; an Arab settlement to the northeast that until the Six-Day War of June 1967 was part of Jordan; and the walled city of Old Jerusalem, also formerly held by Jordan.

To gain entrance to Old Jerusalem, a visitor must pass through one of the seven gates that pierce its wall. On its northern side are the Damascus, New, and Herod's gates; to the east is Saint Stephen's Gate; to the south, the Dung and Zion gates; and on the west is Jaffa Gate.

Within the walls four distinct ethnic and religious communities flourish. The Jewish sector, once the largest settlement in Old Jerusalem, lies just inside the southern wall. During the 1948–49 Arab-Israeli War, the enclave was the scene of heavy fighting that destroyed many of its ancient synagogues and homes. At the close of the war, Old Jerusalem remained under Jordanian control, and most of the Jewish population fled their homes. Recently plans were formulated by the Israeli government to restore the shattered area as a Jewish settlement.

The largest quarter, both in population and in area, is the Moslem sector. Their settlement is adjacent to the Haram Ash-Sharif and dotted by numerous small mosques and active markets.

The Latin and Greek Orthodox Christian quarter occupies the northwest corner of the city and surrounds the chief Christian holy place in Jerusalem, the Church of the Holy Sepulcher. The church is the seat of the Greek Orthodox patriarchate, whose leader heads the largest Christian sect in the Middle East. The Latin patriarchate was established in 1099 by the soldiers of the First Crusade, although the Latin church itself had been active in Jerusalem from a much earlier date.

The southwest corner of Old Jerusalem is known as the Armenian quarter. This section, smallest of the four, is dominated by the Armenian patriarchate and ancient Saint James's Church, a magnificently tiled church built in the Crusader period.

The two-and-a-half-mile perimeter of today's walled city touches only certain sections of ancient Jerusalem; the Jebusite city at Ophel that David conquered around 1000 B.C. lies completely outside its boundaries to the southeast. Archaeological excavations undertaken in the 1960's by the British School of Archaeology, the French Dominican Archaeological School, and the Royal Ontario Museum have enabled us to trace the topography of Jerusalem more closely than ever before.

Old Jerusalem sits on the slopes of two hills: on the west it is bordered by the valley of Hinnom; on the east, by the Kidron valley. As they pass the city, these valleys bend toward each other, forming the city's southern boundary. Running through the center of Jerusalem is a third valley, the Tyropoean, which is entirely filled in by silt deposits so that the city appears to have been built on a plateau.

The original settlement rose on the Ophel ridge, close to the only source of fresh water in the area, the Gihon Spring. It expanded when Solomon built the first Temple some seven hundred feet north of Ophel, on the eastern hill of today's city. At that time Jerusalem covered only a small slip of land, some three thousand feet in length, that linked the crests of two hills.

In 740 B.C. a new wall had to be constructed to enclose a Jerusalem of greatly increased size. Known simply as the First Wall, it ran west from the Temple area to the western hill (the site of the Citadel), then south and east to link with the settlement on Ophel, forming an irregular square.

The First Wall, destroyed and rebuilt numerous times, stood until Herod redesigned Jerusalem between 25 and 13 B.C. Dominating Herod's rebuilt city was the second Temple, resting on its massive supporting platform, and Antonia Fortress, which housed the Roman garrison. While both buildings stood in the vicinity of the obliterated first Temple, their grandiose size actually extended the complex north and necessitated shifting the wall to enclose them. At the same time, Herod built his three-towered palace on what was then the city's northwest corner.

The Second Wall followed the same route as the First Wall on the city's east, south, and west sides, but swung northeast from the palace to link with Antonia Fortress and the Temple area on the north. This wall lasted until Herod Agrippa succeeded to the throne in A.D. 41. With a vision no less grand than that of his grandfather, Herod Agrippa completely remodeled the city of Jerusalem. A third wall was constructed, and this time the Temple area, once the northernmost section, was shifted to the city's southern perimeter.

Archaeologists have not been able to chart precisely the northern extension of the Third Wall, but they have recently found small sections of it under the Damascus Gate, and they theorize that the Third Wall had roughly the same dimensions as the city's present barrier. These discoveries lend support to the belief that the Church of the Holy Sepulcher is indeed built on the actual spot where Jesus was buried — on land that lay outside the city limits when Jesus was crucified.

The construction initiated by Herod Agrippa never reached fruition, for Jerusalem was sacked and burned in A.D. 70 by Roman armies suppressing a Jewish revolt. After a second insurrection, from A.D. 132 to 135, the Romans attempted to obliterate all memory of Jerusalem by establishing a new city, Aelia Capitolina, on its site. A new wall was constructed, and its quadrilineal design has marked the city's boundaries ever since.

The Roman's precise town plan, implemented by Hadrian, is still evident in Jerusalem, where the major east-west thoroughfares, David Street and the Street of the Chain, and the principal north-south thoroughfare, El-Wad Street, follow paths laid down two millennia ago by Roman civil engineers.

In the sixteenth century, Suleiman the Magnificent supervised a refurbishing of the city's walls. In time the ramparts were completely restored, but their contours, marked by seven gates and thirty-four towers, remained unchanged.

The single most important Christian shrine in Jerusalem is the Church of the Holy Sepulcher — a squat, architecturally unimpressive building. Built on the spot where Jesus purportedly died, was buried, and rose again, the structure transcends its lack of grace and symmetry by the force of its spiritual legacy.

The basilica itself parallels the polyglot nature of Christianity in that it is jointly owned by the Latin, Greek, and Armenian Orthodox churches. Most of its nineteen chapels are under the direction of these groups, but others are maintained by the Coptic, Syrian, and Abyssinian churches. On major holidays the sound of masses being celebrated by these varying denominations, from the noisy and outgoing Armenians to the restrained Latins, gives the church a unique ambience.

The building is divided into three principal sections: the chapels above Calvary; the sepulcher itself; and the Chapel of the Finding of the Cross. Entering the church from the south, one ascends a flight of stairs to the summit of Calvary hill. Another stairway leads into the area of the main rotunda. At its entrance is the Stone of the Anointing, which celebrates the spot where Jesus' body was embalmed and anointed.

Passing the stone, one enters the central portion of the church, the magnificent rotunda that covers Jesus' burial crypt. Abutting the eastern side of the rotunda is a small church built by the Crusaders. The simple design of this structure features a transept, choir, and ambulatory with three chapels on its eastern end — but no nave. Finally, a level below the main sections, is the Chapel of the Finding of the Cross — dedicated to Saint Helena's legendary discovery of the True Cross on which Jesus died. On the wall of the stairway leading to the chapel are thousands of small crosses drawn by Christian pilgrims to mark their journey to the Holy Land.

Today the church is an amalgam of architectural styles, principally Byzantine and Romanesque. The building is enclosed by scaffolding which supports the sections of the church that have been weakened by age and by the artillery shelling that occurred during the 1967 war.

As initially conceived and executed by Constantine in the fourth century, the Church of the Holy Sepulcher consisted of three separate sections: the Anastasis, a rotunda covering the sepulcher; the Martyrion, a rectangularly shaped building housing a central church and smaller chapels; and an open courtyard, between these structures, that enclosed the site of Calvary.

The church that Constantine designed was severely damaged by the Persians in A.D. 614. Modestus, the Greek patriarch, authorized a restoration attempt in 628, but he was unable to complete it for lack of funds. Moslems won control of Jerusalem in the late seventh century, and the Church of the Holy Sepulcher suffered periodic acts of desecration at their hands. However, the church continued to function until 1009, when, under orders of the fanatical caliph al-Hakim, the entire building was destroyed. The Moslem leaders who followed al-Hakim displayed more tolerance toward Christianity, and they eventually allowed a new church to be constructed on the site. In 1048, under the direction of Emperor Constantine Monomachus, a new rotunda and an adjacent, modestly sized church were raised.

It was left to the Crusaders who entered Jerusalem in 1099 to restore the structure to some semblance of its earlier dignity. The aim of their design was to enclose the sites of the Passion and the Resurrection under one roof. A building successfully achieving that goal was consecrated in 1141, and it forms the skeleton of today's church. Inevitably, some changes were wrought as the structure was restored following earthquakes in 1545, 1927, and 1937, and a major fire in 1808.

Christian pilgrims customarily make their way to the Church of the Holy Sepulcher by a time-honored route, pausing at holy sites along the Via Dolorosa or Street of Sorrows. By following this path to each of its fourteen "stations," the pilgrim can re-create the journey that Jesus made to Calvary.

The Via Dolorosa's importance to Christians stems from the devotions made by the millions of pilgrims who have walked the winding street, rather than from its historical accuracy. A record of the actual route that Jesus followed was lost in the turbulence of early Christian history, and the path walked today has its origins in the fourth century. In the fifteenth century the Franciscans, designated by the pope as guardians of the Christian holy places in Jerusalem, developed a devotional ritual that included nine stops on the road to Calvary. Five more of these stations were added to the regimen in the eighteenth century to conform with contemporary devotional services in Europe.

Today the route begins in the courtyard of an old Turkish barracks, across from the Convent of the Sisters of Zion. From this spot a pilgrim can see the northwest section of the Temple area — the site, in ancient times, of Antonia Fortress, where Jesus is believed to have been tried and sentenced by Pontius Pilate. The pilgrim then descends a stairway that brings him to street level (paralleling Jesus' descent from Antonia). At this point the Via Dolorosa runs west, passing under Hadrian's Arch and past the Greek Orthodox shrine known as the "Prison of the Christ." On the left is a small Polish chapel marking the Third Station, the spot where Jesus fell for the first time. A few steps south is the Fourth Station, where legend claims that Jesus saw his mother among the crowd watching his journey. An Armenian church marks the site.

The Via Dolorosa then turns west again, passing the Fifth Station, which is called "Simon of Cyrene helps Jesus carry his Cross." The Sixth Station, "Veronica wipes the face of Jesus," is the residence of the Little Sisters of Charles Foucauld, who celebrate their faith by living among the poor of Jerusalem and literally wiping the dirt of the city from their faces.

The Seventh Station, "Jesus falls the second time," is marked by a Franciscan chapel a few blocks further west. A stone plaque set into a wall of the Greek Orthodox Convent of Saint Charalambas commemorates the Eighth Station, "Jesus speaks to the daughters of Jerusalem." The Ninth Station, "Jesus falls for the third time," abuts a Coptic church and is the final station before the pilgrim enters the Church of the Holy Sepulcher.

Within the church are the remaining five stations, beginning with the Tenth Station, "Jesus is stripped of his clothes," in the Chapel of Calvary. This chapel contains two altars: a Latin altar stands upon the Eleventh Station, "Jesus is nailed to the Cross," and a Greek altar marks the Twelfth Station, "Jesus dies on the Cross." The Thirteenth Station, "Jesus is taken down from the Cross," is situated between the two altars. The Fourteenth and final station of the Cross is, of course, the tomb of Jesus in the rotunda of the church.

The simple and austere Church of Saint Anne, situated due north of the Haram, has stood virtually unchanged since the twelfth century. Built in Romanesque style by the Crusaders, the church stands on the supposed site of the house of Joachim and Anna, parents of the Virgin Mary. The church recently underwent extensive repairs for damage caused during the 1967 war.

Standing just south of the Jaffa Gate is the Citadel, a fortress and palace built by Herod and destroyed by Titus. This rectangular structure originally featured three towers, of which only the Tower of Phasael, known today as the David Tower, remains. The Citadel, which occupied a strategically important spot along the perimeter of Aelia Capitolina, was consequently rebuilt by Hadrian. In the twelfth century the fortress was refurbished by Saladin, and it was later renovated by both the Mamelukes and the Turks.

The Haram Ash-Sharif, which dominates the topography of Old Jerusalem and occupies one-sixth of its area, is in turn dominated by the Dome of the Rock. But the Haram, the most sacred Moslem area outside of Mecca and Medina, contains other important religious and historical buildings as well. Al-Aksa, the largest mosque in Jerusalem, stands at the southern end of the Haram on a site consecrated by Moslems about A.D. 700. Between 1938 and 1943 the building was extensively refurbished — the walls rebuilt and the dome repaired — by the Egyptian government. Beneath al-Aksa are vaults, constructed by Herod in the first century B.C., that were later used by the Knights Templar to stable their horses — vaults that they inaccurately dubbed Solomon's Stables.

A few steps east of the Dome of the Rock is the Dome of the Chain, built in the tenth century. Its decorative material and pulpit were added by the Mamelukes. The Dome of the Ascension stands on the spot where Mohammed prayed before his Night Journey to heaven. Its date of construction is not known, but the present six-pillared mosque dates from a reconstruction completed in 1220. To the southwest is An-Nahawia, built in 1270. Originally a school, it now houses a library operated by the Supreme Moslem Council.

To Jews the most sacred site in Jerusalem is the Western Wall, a small remnant of the fortifications that once surrounded the second Temple. Since Byzantine times Jewish custom has directed the faithful to pray daily at the Wall, and their mournful chants and prayers prompted visitors to call it the Wailing Wall. In the twentieth century, rising antagonism between Jews and Arabs sparked a succession of violent disputes over access to the Wall and its surrounding area. After the 1948 war Jordan barred all worship at the Wall, and it was not until 1967, in the wake of the Six-Day War, that Jews were able to resume their daily prayers at this most hallowed site.

Selected Bibliography

Aref al-Aref. *The Dome of the Rock*. Jerusalem: The Commercial Press, 1951.

Avi-Yonah, Michael, ed. *A History of the Holy Land*. London: Weidenfeld & Nicolson Ltd., 1969.

Besant, W., and Palmer, E. H. *Jerusalem*. London: Chatto & Windus Ltd., 1908.

Brilliant, Moshe. *Portrait of Israel*. New York: New York Times/American Heritage Press, 1970.

Cragg, Kenneth. *The Dome and the Rock*. Cairo: S.P.C.K. Press, 1964.

Hitti, Philip K. *History of the Arabs*. London: Macmillan Co. Ltd., 1970.

Kolleck, Teddy, and Pearlman, Moshe. *Jerusalem*. London: Weidenfeld & Nicolson Ltd., 1968.

———. *Pilgrims to the Holy Land*. London: Weidenfeld & Nicolson Ltd., 1970.

Holt, P. M.; Lambton, Ann S.; and Lewis, Bernard, eds. *The Cambridge History of Islam*. Vols. I and II. London: Cambridge University Press, 1970.

Landay, Jerry M. *Silent Cities, Sacred Stones*. New York: McCall's Publishers Inc., 1971.

Parrot, Andre. *The Temple of Jerusalem*. London: SCM Press, 1957.

Perowne, Stewart. *In Jerusalem and Bethlehem*. London: Hodder & Stoughton Ltd., 1964.

Runciman, Sir Steven. *A History of the Crusades*. 3 vols. London: Cambridge University Press, 1954.

Acknowledgments and Picture Credits

The Editors make grateful acknowledgment for the use of excerpted material from the following works:

The Autobiography of Ousama by Ousama Ibn Mounkidh. Translated by George Richard Potter. Copyright 1929 by George Richard Potter. The excerpt appearing on page 148 is reproduced by permission of Routledge & Kegan Paul Ltd.

Old-New Land by Theodor Herzl. Translated by Lotta Levensohn. Copyright 1960 by Bloch Publishing Co. The excerpt appearing on page 156 is reproduced by permission of Bloch Publishing Co.

The New Jerusalem by G. K. Chesterton. Copyright 1948 by Dorothy E. Collins. The excerpt appearing on pages 157–58 is reproduced by permission of Dorothy E. Collins.

Swift Sword by S. L. A. Marshall. Copyright 1967 by American Heritage Publishing Co. and United Press International. The excerpt appearing on pages 158–60 is reproduced by permission of American Heritage Publishing Co.

The Editors would like to express their particular appreciation to Marvin E. Newman of New York for his creative photography in Jerusalem and to Ellen Kavier of New York, who wrote Guide to Old Jerusalem *on pages 165–67. In addition, the Editors would like to thank the following organizations and individuals:*

Consulate General of Israel — Nahum Eshkol, Gabriel Padon

Marilyn Flaig, New York

Lydia Hancock, Rome

Hill & Knowlton, Inc., New York — David Snyder

Kate Lewin, Paris

Barbara Nagelsmith, Paris

Spencer Collection, New York Public Library — Elizabeth Roth

Susan Storer, New York

The title or description of each picture appears after the page number (boldface), followed by its location. Photographic credits appear in parentheses. The following abbreviations are used:

BN,P   — Bibliothèque Nationale, Paris
BM   — British Museum, London
(MEN)   — (Marvin E. Newman)
SC(NYPL) — Spencer Collection. New York Public Library, Geoffrey Clements

ENDPAPERS Gold and mosaic ceiling of the Dome of the Rock (MEN)   HALF TITLE Symbol designed by Jay J. Smith Studio   FRONTISPIECE Miniature of the Ascension of Mohammed, from a 16th-century Persian manuscript. Collection Trunifer, Lucerne (Giraudon)   9 Tiles from the exterior of the Dome of the Rock (MEN)   10 German engraving showing Jerusalem as the center of the world, 16th century (The Mansell Collection)   12 Miniature of pilgrims entering Jerusalem, from *Passages d'Outremer*, 15th century. BN,P, Ms. Fr. 9087 fol 85v

CHAPTER I   15 Medallion of Emperor Heraclius's entry into Constantinople with the True Cross, 7th century. Dumbarton Oaks Collection   16 Miniature of the archangel Gabriel preparing Mohammed for his Night Journey, from *Siyar-i Nabi* by Darir, 16th century. fol 3r. SC(NYPL)   17 Miniature of the Ascension of Mohammed, from *Khamseh* by Nizami, 16th century. BM, Ms. Or. 2265 fol 195a   19 Map of the Middle East by Francis & Shaw, Inc.   20–21 Dawn at the Dome of the Rock (MEN)   24–25 left, Jews at the Wailing Wall; middle, Arabs at the Temple Mount; right, Christians on the Via Dolorosa (MEN)

CHAPTER II   27 Stele showing warfare, *c.* 2300 B.C. Louvre   28 Miniature of the Throne of Mercy, from a 13th-century Hebrew prayer book. BM, Ms. Or. Add. 11639 fol 522   29 Miniature of David bringing the Ark of the Covenant into Jerusalem, from a 12th-century English Bible. Bodleian Library, Oxford Ms. Laud. Misc. 752 fol 279v   30 Ivory panel of cherubim, from the North-West Palace, Nimrud, 8th century B.C. BM   31 Basin stand from Cyprus. BM (Michael Holford)   32 Miniature of David enthroned with his son Solomon, from a Byzantine manuscript. Vatican Library, Ms. Grec. 699 fol 63v   34 top, Miniature of Nebuchadnezzar taking Jerusalem; bottom, Miniature of Pompey desecrating Solomon's Temple. Both by Jean Fouquet, from *Antiquités des Juifs* by Flavius Josephus, 1470. BN,P, Ms. Fr. 247 fol 213v and 293v   35 Miniature of Cyrus granting clemency to the ten tribes of Israel, by Jean Fouquet, from *Antiquités des Juifs*, by Flavius Josephus, 1470. BN,P, Ms. Fr. 247 fol 230v   36 Detail of the revolt of the Maccabees, from *Bible de Rodas*, 10th century. BN,P, Ms. Lat. 6 (111) fol 145   37 Miniature of Herod directing the slaughter of the children of Bethlehem, from *Tropaire d'Autun*, 11–12th century. Bibliothèque de l'Arsenal, Paris, Ms. 1169 fol 11   38 top, Inscription from second Temple. Israel Department of Antiquities and Museums; bottom, Model of second Temple by Professor Michael Avi-Yonah. Holyland Hotel, Jerusalem (MEN)   39 Excavations in Herod's Upper City (MEN)   41 top, Miniature of Jesus entering Jerusalem; bottom, Miniature of Jesus before Pontius Pilate. Both from *Evangelisto Siriaco di Rossano Calabro*, 6th century. Both: Museo dell' Arcivescovado, Rossano (Mauro Pucciarelli)   42 top, Coin of Vespasian; bottom left, Coin of the destruction of the Temple, "*Judaea Capta*"; bottom right, Coin of the façade of the Temple. American Numismatic Society   44 Detail of the spoils of Jerusalem, from the Arch of Titus in Rome (Alinari)   45 Arab Miniature of the destruction of the Temple. Edinburgh University Library, Arabic Ms. 161 fol 134v

CHAPTER III   47 Monogram of Christ, 6–7th century, Syria. Cleveland Museum of Art   48 Miniature of Constantine killing his enemies, from a manuscript made in Constantinople, 1066. BM, Ms. Add. 19352 fol 75   49 Coin of Helena. Dumbarton Oaks Collection   50 Interior of the Church of the Holy Sepulcher (MEN)   51 top right, Entrance to the *ædicula* in the Church of the Holy Sepulcher; top left, Station of the Cross in the Church of the Holy Sepulcher; bottom, Site of Golgotha in the Church of the Holy Sepulcher (MEN)   52 Stone of the Anointing in the Church of the Holy Sepulcher (MEN)   53 top, Entrance to the Arab sweetshop that stands on the site of the original entrance to the Church of the Holy Sepulcher; bottom, Remnants of the original entrance to the Church of the Holy Sepulcher (MEN)   54–55 Fresco of Helena discovering the Three Crosses of Golgotha. Church of SS. Quattro Coronati, Rome (Mauro Pucciarelli)   56 Bust of the Empress Theodora, *c.* 530. Museo Castello Sforzesco, Milan   57 Medallion of Justinian, 534–38. BM   58–59 Enamel of Heraclius killing Khosrau II, 13th century. Louvre

CHAPTER IV   61 Stele of an Arab and his camels from South Arabia, 1st century A.D. Louvre   62 Miniature of Ali answering questions about Mohammed at the Kaaba, from *Sivar-i Nabi* by Darir, 16th century. fol 333v. SC(NYPL)   63 Miniature of Mohammed rededicating the Black Stone at the Kaaba, from *Jami Al-Tawarikh*, by Rashid Al-Din, 1314. Edinburgh University Library, Ms. 20 fol 55   64 Miniature of Mohammed building a mosque in Medina   65 Miniature of the unbelievers stoning Mohammed, who is protected by Abu Bakr. Both from *Sivar-i Nabi*, by Darir, 16th century. fol 356v and fol 136r. SC(NYPL)   67 The Dome of the Chain (MEN)   68 The interior of the dome of the Church of the Holy Sepulcher (MEN)   69 The interior of the dome of the Dome of the Rock (MEN)   70 Two diagrams of the Dome of the Rock. Francis & Shaw, Inc.   71 Diagram of the Church of the Holy Sepulcher. Francis & Shaw, Inc.   72–73 Interior of the Dome of the Rock (MEN)   74 Arab women praying in the Dome of the Rock (MEN)   76–77 Jerusalem from the Mount of Olives (MEN)

CHAPTER V   79 Norse chesspiece of a medieval knight, *c.* 1200. National Museum of Antiquities of Scotland   80 Miniature from the *Roman de Godfrey de Bouillon*. BN,P, Ms. Fr. 22495 fol 9   81 Miniature of the Council of Clermont, from *Passages d'Outremer*, 15th century. BN,P, Ms.

Fr. 5594 fol 19 **84** top, Miniature of the epidemic during the siege of Antioch; bottom, Miniature of the siege of Antioch. Both from the *Histoire de Jerusalem* by Guillaume de Tyr, 13th century. BN,P, Ms. Fr. 9081 fols 65 and 44 **85** Jerusalem from Nabi Samwil (MEN) **86** Crusader map of Jerusalem, 12th century. Bibliothèque Royale, Brussels, Ms. 9823–34, fol 157r **88** Miniature of the siege of Jerusalem, from *Chroniques d'Outremer* by Godfrey de Bouillon. BN,P, Ms. Fr. 352, fol 62 **90** Basilica of the Ascension. (MEN) **91** Mosaic of Christ on a ceiling vault in the Church of the Holy Sepulcher (MEN)

CHAPTER VI **93** Seal of the Knights Templar, 1255. BM **94** Interior of the Dome of the Rock (MEN) **95** Woodcut of Baldwin II in 1247, from *Historia Byzantina*, 1680. BM **97** Detail of the Temple, from *The Marriage of the Virgin* by Raphael, 1504. Brera, Milan **98** Miniature of Saladin defeating the Christians **99** Miniature of two Knights Templar on a horse. Both from *Historia Major* by Matthew Paris. Corpus Christi College, Cambridge, Ms. 26 (Bodleian filmstrip 178) **100–101** The Field of Hattin (MEN) **101** left, Miniature of Moslems defending a tower; right, Miniature of Moslems and Christians in battle. Both from *Roman de Godfrey de Bouillon*. BN,P, Ms. Fr. 22495 fol 30 and fol 265v **104** Exterior of al-Aksa **105** Interior of al-Aksa (Both: MEN)

CHAPTER VII **107** Ottoman rosette from the Damascus Gate (MEN) **108** One of the Dome's four minarets, from the Temple Mount (MEN) **109** left, One of the four minarets, from the Temple Mount; right, The *sabil* of Qaitbay (MEN) **110** Coin of Mohammed II, by Costanzo de Ferrara. BM **111** The ablution fountain between al-Aksa and the Dome of the Rock (MEN) **112** Turkish miniature of Ottoman armies campaigning, 16th century. Topkapi Palace Museum (Ara Guler) **114–15** Two doors of the Dome of the Rock (MEN) **116–17** Four views of the Damascus Gate (MEN) **118–19** Stained-glass and mosaic tilework on interior of the Dome of the Rock (MEN) **120** Interior of the Dome of the Rock (MEN) **122–23** Gold and mosaic ceiling of the Dome of the Rock

CHAPTER VIII **125** Miniature of a menorah from a Haggadah. BM, Ms. Add. 15250 fol 3v **126** Tiles from the exterior of the Dome of the Rock (MEN) **127** The Dome of the Rock prior to renovation. Central Zionist Archives **129** Map of Palestine and Jerusalem by Rabbi Haim Shelomo Pinie, 1875. Maritime Museum, Haifa **130** Sir Edmund Allenby and British forces entering Jerusalem, 1917. Central Zionist Archives **133** Israeli soldiers rejoicing at Dome of the Rock after the Six-Day War of June 1967. (Cornell Capa, Magnum) **134** Israeli soldiers at the Wailing Wall after the Six-Day War, 1967. (Cornell Capa, Magnum) **135** left, The pulpit of Nureddin in al-Aksa; right, al-Aksa smoldering after the fire set by Denis Michael Rohan, 1969 (Wide World)

JERUSALEM IN LITERATURE **136** Miniature of Moslems, Jews, and Christians in Abraham's lap, from the *Bible de Souvigny*, 12th century. Bibliothèque des Moulins (Giraudon) **139–59** Lithographs by W. H. Bartlett, from *Walks about the City and Environs of Jerusalem*, London, 1843.

REFERENCE **164** Map by Francis & Shaw, Inc.

Index